**Jemma Kennedy**

# The Prince and the Pauper

*based on the novel by Mark Twain*

**Methuen Drama**

**Bloomsbury**

**Methuen Drama**

An imprint of Bloomsbury Publishing Plc

50 Bedford Square        175 Fifth Avenue
London        New York
WC1B 3DP        NY 10010
UK        USA

**www.bloomsbury.com**

First published 2012

ISBN
PB: 978-1-472-51563-6
ePDF: 978-1-472-51565-0
ePub: 978-1-472-51564-3

A CIP catalogue record for this book
is available from the British Library.

Typeset by Country Setting, Kingsdown, Kent

# The Prince and the Pauper

*by*
*Mark Twain*

*adapted by*
*Jemma Kennedy*

*The Prince and the Pauper*
was first performed at the Unicorn Theatre
on Friday 30 November 2012

# UNICORN

## The UK's leading theatre for young audiences

The Unicorn Theatre is the UK's leading theatre for young audiences, serving over 70,000 children, young people and families every year through its professional performances, participation and other events.

Founded in 1947 by Caryl Jenner, the company originally operated out of the back of a van, and touring theatre for children into schools and community centres. The Unicorn was subsequently based at the Arts Theatre in London's West End for many years, before moving into its current home at London Bridge in 2005. Today, the Unicorn building has two theatres, two rehearsal rooms and four floors of public space dedicated to producing and presenting work for audiences aged 2 to 21.

It is a central part of the Unicorn's mission to commission new work, to tour, to be accessible to all and to encourage exchange and collaboration between theatre-makers from different countries and traditions, coming together to develop ideas and projects.

**unicorntheatre.com**

Box Office 020 7645 0560
147 Tooley Street, London SE1 2HZ

Charity number: 225751
Company number: 480920

### Thanks to

The Williams Charitable Trust, The John Ellerman Foundation,
The Goods, Denise and Arnold Holle, Farida Ghwedar, Martina Trottmann,
Charlotte Young, Tete Pocas, Annike Flo, Angela Sanchez del Campo,
Gyo Kim, Paul Marneur and Marius Bogdanas

Supported using public funding by
**ARTS COUNCIL
ENGLAND**

LOTTERY FUNDED

**Artistic Director**   Purni Morell
**Executive Director**   Anneliese Davidsen

ARTISTIC AND ADMINISTRATION
**Programme Producer**   Carolyn Forsyth
**Finance Manager**   Amanda Koch-Schick
**Learning Associate**   Catherine Greenwood
**Young Company Director**   Ellen Edwin-Scott
**Learning and Participation Manager**   Jenny Maddox (Maternity Leave)
**General Administrator**   Jenny Skene

DEVELOPMENT
**Director of Development**   Dorcas Morgan
**Development Managers**
Alex Jones, Marylka Gowlland (Maternity Leave), Caroline Darke (Maternity Cover)
**Development Officer**   Melissa Wilkins

MARKETING & COMMUNICATIONS
**Communications Consultant**   Heather Clark-Charrington
**Access Manager**   Kirsty Hoyle
**Marketing Coordinators**   Isabel Madgwick & Bonnie Smith
**Schools Relationship Manager**   Ella MacFadyen
**Front of House Manager**   Sair Smith
**Box Office Manager**   Helen Corbett

**Performance Managers**
Lewis Church, Joycelyn Chung, Lyn Medcalf, Laura Standen

**Ushers**
Euan Borland, Philip Moore, Chris MaCallister, Clare Quinn, Francesca Turauskis,
Henry Reynolds, Housni Hassan, Jackie Downer, Kathryn Tighe, Krystal Boyde-Maynard,
Laura Standen, Lyn Medcalf, Marie-Louise O'Connor, Matthew Newell, Miles Yekinni,
Nathan Rumney, Rachel Roberts, Rebecca Walker, Robert Weaver, Thomas Dancaster

**Box Office Assistants**
Euan Borland, Laura Fiesco (Maternity Leave), Nadia Giscir, Julia Hayes,
Phil Moore, Amy Mulholland, Clare Quinn, Claire Sundin, Martin Walsh

TECHNICAL
**Technical Director**   Phil Clarke
**Technical Stage Manager**   Andy Shewan
**Stage Technician**   Jeff Mitchell
**Sound Technician**   Keith Edgehill
**Lighting Technician**   Shane Burke
**Building Technician**   Martin Turner
**Company & Stage Manager**   Richard Pattison
**Deputy Stage Manager**   Kathryn Linnel
**Assistant Stage Manager**   Louise Lofthouse
**Stage Door Supervisors**
Paul Brewster, John Cockerill, Sidonie Ferguson, Alice Malseed

BOARD
Joanna Kennedy (Chair), Denise Holle, Richard Hope, Carolyn Maddox, Bryan Savery,
Sarah West, Richard Oldfield, John Langley, Giles Havergal

YOUTH BOARD
Natalie Soobhee-Nelson, Maria Ratsevits, Kianna Witter-Prendergast, Daniel Curthoys,
Douglas Wood, Florence Dessau, Oliver Simpson, Klajdi Selimi

## JEMMA KENNEDY

Jemma Kennedy was Pearson Playwright at the National Theatre Studio in 2010 and part of the inaugural Soho 6 writing scheme with the Soho Theatre Company in 2011. Plays include *The Seagull* (adaptation, Tabard Theatre); *How To Remember the Dead* (Radio 4 Afternoon Play); *The Grand Irrationality* (Lost Theatre Studio, Los Angeles) and *Don't Feed the Animals* for National Theatre Connections 2013. Her first novel *Skywalking* was published by Viking Penguin in 2003 and she has three films in development with Objective Productions and Focus Features. Jemma is also a writing tutor and a mentor for the Koestler Foundation. She recently wrote the National Theatre's New Views online playwriting course for young writers.

## SELINA CARTMELL

Selina holds an MA (Distinction) from Central School of Speech & Drama in Advanced Theatre Practice in Directing and a First Class MA in History of Art and Drama from Trinity College, Dublin and Glasgow University. She is Artistic Director of award winning company Siren Productions and has recently been made Artist-In-Residence at the Samuel Beckett Theatre, Dublin.

For Siren Productions she directed the World Premiere of Robin Robertson's new translation of *Medea* (winner of the Best Director Award and nominated for 5 Irish Times Theatre Awards 2011 including Best Production and Best Actress); *Macbeth*; the award winning *Titus Andronicus* (winner of 4 Irish Times Theatre Awards including Best Production and Best Director); *La Musica* (Best Production and Best Actress – Dublin Fringe Festival); *Fando & Lis* and *Shutter* (Project Arts Centre). Other recent productions include *Woman and Scarecrow* (Abbey Theatre); *Sweeney Todd* (Gate Theatre, Best Opera Production at the 2008 Irish Times Theatre Awards); *Festen* and *Catastrophe* (Beckett Centenary Festival 2007 (Barbican); *Molly Sweeney* as part of the Friel Festival (Curve, Leicester); Marina Carr's *The Cordelia Dream* for the Royal Shakespeare Company at Wilton's Music Hall and *The Giant Blue Hand* for The Ark, Dublin. In January 2012, Selina directed *The Broken Heart* for Theatre For A New Audience in New York (nominated for a Lucille Lortel Award). Selina will be directing *King Lear* for the Abbey Theatre in February 2013.

In 2007 Selina was chosen as a Protégé in the third cycle of the *Rolex Mentor and Protégé Arts Initiative*, an international philanthropic programme that pairs rising young creatives with master artists for a year of mentoring. Selina's mentor was world-renowned director and designer Julie Taymor.

## GARANCE MARNEUR

Based in London, Garance is a dedicated and driven Live Performance Designer, producing innovative and creative sets and costumes for both theatre, dance and opera in the UK and Internationally.

Garance studied Fine Art in Paris and graduated with first class honours in Design for Performance at Central Saint Martins in London, where she now works as a Visiting Practitioner. Her recent work includes *Tenet* (Gate Theatre); *The Legend of Captain Crow's Teeth* (Unicorn Theatre); *Herding Cats* (Hampstead Theatre Downstairs); *Measure for Measure* and *Marat Sade* (Royal Shakespeare Company); *Sold* (Theatre 503); a national tour of *Khaos* (Scottish Dance Theatre); *Herding Cats, The Chairs* and *Gagarin Way* (Theatre Royal Bath); *Rhetoric, My Arm, What Would Judas Do?, A Prayer* and *Tonight David Ireland Will Lecture Dance and Box* (Greyscale) and the national tours of *Huck* and *Romeo and Juliet* (Ballet-Switzerland).

Garance was the 2007 overall winner of the Linbury Biennial Prize for Stage Design held at the National Theatre in London. She has also been nominated for the Most Successful Freelancer Award, Creative Enterprise Awards 2009 & 2010.

## CHAHINE YAVROYAN

Chahine's recent theatre includes: *The Kitchen Sink* (Hull Truck); *The Astronaut's Chair* (The Drum); *A Soldier In Every Son* (RSC); *The House* (The Abbey, Dublin); *Uncle Vanya* (Chichester); *Someone Who'll Watch Over Me* (Perth Theatre); *Nora* (Belgrade B2); *Measure for Measure* and *Marat/Sade* (RSC); *Tuesday at Tesco's* (Assembly Hall, Edinburgh); *Glorious* (Spill Festival); *Bronte* (Shared Experience); *Dunsinane, Little Eagles* (RSC at Hampstead Theatre); *Scorched* (Old Vic Tunnels); *Dr Marigold & Mr Chops* (Riverside); *1984* (Blind Summit at BAC); *Orphans* (Paines Plough/Soho); *Dr Faustus, Fuente Ovejuna, Il Castigo Sin Vengansa* (Madrid); *Damascus* (Traverse/Tricycle/Middle East); *Relocated, Wig Out!, Get Santa* (Royal Court); *God in Ruins* (RSC at Soho Theatre); *Three Sisters, Comedy of Errors, The Lady From The Sea* (Royal Exchange); *Dallas Sweetman* (Paines Plough/Canterbury Cathedral); *Sun & Heir* (ROH/Tilbury Cruise Terminal); *Fall* (Traverse); *Il Tempo Del Postino* (MIF/Manchester Opera House); *The Wonderful World of Dissocia* (National Theatre of Scotland/Royal Court) and countless productions for People Show.

Her dance work includes working with Jasmin Vardimon, Frauke Requardt, Arthur Pita, CanDoCo, Bock & Vincenzi etc. Her music work includes *XX Scharnhorst for Thames Festival* (HMS Belfast); *Home & Sevastopol for Operashots '12* (ROH2); *Diamanda Galas* (RFH & International); *Dalston Songs* (ROH2); *Plague Songs* (Barbican Hall) and *Fables* (Streetwise Opera).

Chahine has also worked on fashion shows with Clemens Ribeiro, Givenchy, Chalayan and Ghost.

*The Prince and the Pauper* in rehearsal, November 2012.

*The Prince and the Pauper* in rehearsal, November 2012.

## TOM CURRAN

Tom trained as a Chorister at St John's College Cambridge, and is currently studying Composition at the Guildhall School of Music & Drama. In 2008 he was one of the winners of the BBC Proms Young Composers Competition and was subsequently commissioned to write music for the 2009 Proms. Tom has worked composing, arranging, playing and producing music for the stage, screen and concert hall, and is a member of the National Youth Theatre Production Department.

Credits as Musical Director include: *Dick Whittington* (Chelmsford); *The Queen of Hearts, Letters to Myself* (Tristan Bates Theatre); *The Sword in the Stone* (UK tour); *After the Turn* (Courtyard Theatre); *FRESHER the Musical* (Pleasance Dome, Edinburgh); *Wind in the Willows* (Musical Supervisor - UK tour). Assistant MD credits include: *Plug in the Lead, West End Unplugged* (Leicester Square Theatre); *The Producers* (Arts Ed); *In Town with Motown, Mash Up Cabaret* (Paulden Hall Productions); *Hello, Jerry!* (Landor Theatre); *Robin Hood, Alice's Adventures in Wonderland* (UK tours).

Orchestration credits include: *My Land's Shore [Workshop]*; *Peter Pan [workshop]* (Lyric Theatre); *Jekyll & Hyde* (Union Theatre); *After the Turn* (Courtyard Theatre). Film composition credits include: *Henry Morris - The Life & Legacy* (Heritage Lottery); *It's All About Us!* (Cambridgeshire County Council); *Projecting the Past* (Stories - Projects in Film).

For more information please visit www.tomcurran.co.uk

## SUSAN KULKARNI

Susan is currently Head of Costume for Secret Cinema and Future Cinema and designs all of their global events including the recent critically acclaimed *Prometheus* and *Bugsy Malone*. She has costume designed many shows at the National Theatre including *Detroit, Cesario* and *Prince of Denmark*, she has also designed for and worked on shows for Punchdrunk, ITV, BBC, the ENO, the RSC and Laban. Most recently, she worked as part of the costume team on *Downton Abbey* and *Dancing on the Edge* directed by Stephen Poliakoff.

Susan read English at Somerville College, Oxford University and then undertook a postgraduate course in Costume at RADA.

## ANTONY ELVIN

Antony Elvin is a singer/songwriter/composer and musical comedian.

He is one half of Hot Brew, a comedy double-act with Perrier Award-winning actor Alice Lowe (*Sightseers, Garth Merenghi, The Harry and Paul Show*). His song, *Among the Dandies* features in the Mighty Boosh film *Journey of the Childmen*. He has made music for mayonnaise adverts and many short films. Antony is a member of the music trio *Princes in the Tower* playing Medieval/Renaissance music and delivering Tudor music workshops in schools and historical sites. They recently appeared with their music in Julia Davis' Sky Atlantic series *Hunderby*. Antony also writes songs for children, in collaboration with award-winning arts education company Artburst, which are used in the V&A Museum of Childhood Wondertots sessions

## KATE WATERS

Kate is one of only two women on the Equity Register of Fight Directors.

Her extensive work for the National Theatre includes: *The Curious Incident of the Dog in the Night-Time; The Comedy of Errors; One Man, Two Guvnors (also West End); Frankenstein; Seasons Greetings; Hamlet; Twelfth Night; Welcome to Thebes; Women Beware Women* and *War Horse* (also West End).

Her other recent work includes: *Cabaret* (West End); *Noises Off* (Old Vic & West End); *Duchess of Malfi* (Old Vic); *Written On Skin* (Aix En Provence & Royal Opera House 2013, for Katie Mitchell); *Company* (Sheffield Crucible); *Henry 1V Part 1 & 2* ( Bath Theatre Royal, Peter Hall Co); *Richard III, Henry V & Dr Faustus* (The Globe); *A Midsummer Night's Dream, Ragtime & Lord of the Flies* (Regents Park); *The House of Bernarda Alba* (Almeida); *The Homecoming, King Lear & American Trade* (RSC); *Our New Girl* (Bush Theatre); *Saturday Night, Sunday Morning, Private Lives, A View The From Bridge, As You Like It* (Royal Exchange, Manchester); *King Lear* ( West Yorkshire Playhouse); *Desire Under The Elms, Saved, The Chair Plays, Blasted & Twisted Tales* (Lyric Theatre, Hammersmith); *Communicating Doors & Carmen* (Stephen Joseph Theatre & Tour); *A View From The Bridge* (Theatre by the Lake, Keswick) and *Great Expectations* (ETT & Watford Palace Theatre).

Kate regularly coordinates the fight direction for Coronation Street and has also been interviewed on Woman's Hour and Midweek for Radio 4 and has been featured in The Sunday Times Culture Section.

## DANIELLE BIRD

Danielle Bird graduated from Mountview Academy of Theatre Arts in 2009. Danielle is no stranger to working alongside her twin sister, Nichole, most recently featuring in Mike Leigh's latest film *'A Running Jump'* (BBC Films/Film4). Previous roles together include *The Twisted Sisters* (Colin Hoult's Real Horror Show at Leicester Square Theatre); *Magician's Assistant* (You Me Bum Bum Train); *Indian Ocean* (Yellow Productions); *The Double Life of Morton Coyle* (The Comedy Unit), as well as boggling the crowds as exhibition performers for Damien Hirst (Tate Modern).

Danielle's other work includes *No Ball Games* (New Wolsey Theatre); *As You Like It* (Principal Theatre) and *Romeo and Juliet* and *Hamlet* (Young Shakespeare Company). Danielle also thoroughly enjoyed working on home turf in South Wales with Hijinx Theatre Company.

Danielle also does stilt walking, puppetry and storytelling performances with the circus theatre company Circo Rum Ba Ba and has performed as a wall running aerialist for Scarabeus Aerial Theatre/National Youth Theatre.

**NICHOLE BIRD**

Nichole, originally from South Wales, graduated from Mountview Academy of Theatre Arts in 2009. Her professional debut was as Phoebe in Principle Theatre Company's open-air production of Shakespeare's *As You Like It*. Other classical performances include *Arden of Faversham* (Rose Theatre) and roles with the Young Shakespeare Company.

She has embarked on a UK Tour of *Never Saw The Day* with 'Walking Forward' and a tour of Germany with TNT 's *Death of A Salesman*. Further theatre includes *The Woman Before* at SOHO Studio. She has also worked with comedian Colin Hoult on his *Real Horror Shows* at The Leicester Square Theatre and was involved in the immersive theatre experience *You Me Bum Bum Train*.

Short film work includes *Indian Ocean* and several issue-based films entitled *Untold Stories* for the charity organisation, Media Trust. Most recently Nichole featured inMike Leigh's film *A Running Jump* as part of Festival 2012 and commissioned by LOCOG.

**NICHOLAS BOULTON**

Nicholas trained at the Guildhall School of Music & Drama. His recent theatre work includes: *The Bird and the Two-Ton Weight* (Old Vic, New Voices); *1908: Body and Soul* (Lightning Ensemble/Jacksons Lane); *Private Lives* (Salisbury Playhouse); *Restoration* (Salisbury Arts Theatre); *Mirandolina* (Royal Exchange Theatre); *The Rivals* (National Tour); *The Taming of the Shrew* (National Tour); *Barbarians, Hysteria* (Salisbury Playhouse); *A Chaste Maid in Cheapside and Platonov* (The Almeida).

His recent television includes: *Midsomer Murders* (Bentley Productions); *Hustle* (Kudos); *Doctors XI* (BBC); *Doc Martin* (Buffalo Pictures) and *Jonathan Creek*. Films include: *Expectation Management; Deadly Descent; Arn; Kovak Box; Topsy Turvey* and *Shakespeare in Love*.

Nicholas has also done extensive work in radio and was a member of the BBC Radio Repertory Company, 1993 – 1994.

**RICHARD EVANS**

Richard started acting whilst a student at the University of York. He went on to study singing in London, Hamburg and the Royal Northern College of Music before joining Scottish Opera, the Royal Opera and Glyndebourne Festival Opera. In 1978, he played Joseph Bowman in Patrick Garland's adaptation of Thomas Hardy's *Under The Greenwood Tree* at the Vaudeville Theatre, London, and since then acting has taken him all over the UK.

Recent theatre includes *Dear Father Christmas* (Oxford Playhouse); a national tour of Hamlet (*Northern Broadside)* and *Saturn Returns* (Finborough Theatre). Other theatre includes *The Crucible* (Bolton Octagon); *Burial At Thebes* (Nottingham Theatre and US Tour); *As You Like It* (Derby Playhouse); *No Shame No Fear* (Jermyn Street Theatre); *Macbeth* and *Robin Hood* (Creation Theatre); *As You Like It, Antony and Cleopatra* (English Shakespeare Company National Tour and Perth Festival, Australia); *Beowulf* (English Shakespeare Company); *As You Like It* (Greenwich Playhouse) and *Rosencrantz and Guildenstern are Dead* (Theatre Royal Bury St Edmonds). Television and Film includes *Being Human; The Trip; The Conspiracy Theories; The Pinocchio Effect; The Brief; North and South; Fight to the Death; The Gathering* and *The Inspector Linley Mysteries*. Directing credits include *The Best Little Whorehouse in Texas* and *West Side Story* (Bloomsbury Theatre).

## JONATHAN GLEW

Jon trained at LIPA. His theatre credits include: *She Stoops To Conquer, Jerry Springer – The Opera* (National Theatre); *Masters, Are You Mad?* and *Twelfth Night* (The Grosvenor Park Open Air Theatre); *The Sun and Heir* (The Royal Opera House); *Meditation* (Buddhist Arts Theatre); *Turning Trix* (Landor); *Silence* (Young Vic); Terry Pratchett's *Only You Can Save Mankind: The Musical* (Pleasance, Edinburgh); *Anyone Can Whistle* (Bridewell ) and *Police Story* (SJD). Workshops for the National Theatre Studio include: *Antigone; London Road; Swallows and Amazons; 57 Hours.* Jon also won the Olivier Award for Best Supporting Performance in a Musical for his performance in *Jerry Springer – The Opera.*

Films include: *The Adventures of Dave, Vengeance of Wrath* and *Escape The Night.*

Jonathan has his own band *Four Thousand Islands* and sings with an a capella choir *The Shout*, both of whom tour nationally and internationally.

## JAKE HARDERS

Jake trained at the Grotowski Centre, Poland. His theatre credits include *Beasts and Beauties* (Hampstead Theatre); *Agamemnon* (Cambridge Arts Theatre); *The Crucible* (Teatr Pieśń Kozła, Warsaw); *The Hypochondriac* (Liverpool Playhouse/English Touring Theatre UK tour); *Six Characters in Search of an Author* (Chichester Festival, West End and Australian tour); *Hobson's Choice* (Chichester Festival UK tour); *Rope* (Watermill); *Cymbeline* (Cheek by Jowl world tour – Rolex Mentor-Protégé Award Nomination); *The Comedy of Errors, Titus Andronicus* (Shakespeare's Globe); *Journey's End* (West End); *Professor Bernhardi, Rose Bernd* and *Candida* (Oxford Stage Company – Ian Charleson Award Commendation).

Jake's film, radio and television credits include *Bel Ami; The Picture Man* (BBC)' *Family Tree* (HBO); *Parents, Beethoven, Wannabes* (BBC); *Dark Matters* (Science Channel); *I Shouldn't Be Alive* (Discovery); *Peep Show* (C4), *Foyle's War* (ITV).

## JASON MORELL

Jason trained at Central School of Speech and Drama. His recent theatre credits include *Merchant of Venice* and *The Taming of the Shrew* (RSC); *Oliver!* (Theatre Royal, Drury Lane); *Faustus* (Hampstead Theatre); *Thirteen Objects, Gertrude* (Riverside Studios); *Rainsnakes* (Young Vic); *The Reckless are Dying Out, The Cenci, Hamlet* (Lyric Hammersmith); *The Silver Lake* (Wilton's Music Hall); *Lysistrata* (Arcola); *Swanwhite* (The Gate); *The Difficult Man* and *The Leonardo Project* (National Theatre Studio); *The Critic* (Manchester Royal Exchange); *Ritual in Blood* (Nottingham Playhouse); *The Duchess of Malfi, Romeo and Juliet, The Rehearsal* and *The Double Inconstancy* (Salisbury Playhouse) and *The Artificial Jungle* (Leicester Haymarket). Jason's film credits include *Artefacts, The Gathering; The Lake; Mrs Brown; Wilde; Damage* and *Biddy.* His television credits include *Dr Who; Affinity; Ultimate Force; My Dad's the Prime Minister; Hear the Silence; Father and Daughter; Second Sight-Parasomnia; Aristophanes-the Gods are Laughing* and *The Bill.*

## KATHERINE TOY

Katherine's previous theatre work includes *The Caucasian Chalk Circle* (Shared Experience); *Cyrano de Bergerac, The False Servant* and *Life of Galileo* (National Theatre); *Comedy of Errors* (RSC); *Pool piece* (Oily Cart); *Treasure Island* (Newbury Watermill); *Macbeth* (Southwark Playhouse) *Wild Orchids* (Chichester Festival Theatre) and *Rumpelstiltskin* (Nottingham Playhouse).

Her TV credits include *Waiting for God* and *Our Tune* (BBC) and *Tatort* (German ARD TV). As a musician she has played for 20 years with the speciality act *The Virtuosos* and not quite so long with *Nicetoy*, an Argentine Tango duo. Katherine has toured with Paul Hartnoll of *Orbital, The Real Band* and most recently with *The Shtetl Superstars.*

# What was life like in Tudor London?

London was the largest city in the country, with many people moving there in the hope that its streets would be paved with gold! The population quadrupled from around 50,000 people in 1500 to 200,000 in 1600.

Bankside, pictured in the sixteenth-century engraving on the opposite page (and the area in which the Unicorn Theatre is located today), was one of the most popular parts of London during the late Tudor era. The old London Bridge was the only way to get across the Thames so it was always packed full of people, just like it is today.

In those days, people didn't use Oyster cards to get around London so you had to walk to get anywhere. The narrow and winding streets were very crowded and were often a dangerous place to be. If you were rich you would have been lucky enough to avoid the hustle and bustle and travel by boat along the grimy Thames.

Everyone knows how stroppy Edward's dad, King Henry VIII, could get if someone disobeyed his rules. It's rumoured that he arrested and executed over 72,000 people during his reign, including two of his six wives! In the picture, at the Bankside end of the old London Bridge you can just see the heads of those unfortunate enough to have theirs chopped off, displayed on spikes as a warning to the public not to break the law.

Tudor London was very smelly. It was full to the brim with people who had nowhere to put their waste so it all ended up being dumped in the Thames. Because of this, the City was frequently struck by epidemics of the plague, the most severe occurring in 1665.

The very first theatres in the country were built during the Tudor era and they proved to be extremely popular. Theatres such as the Globe were often packed to the rafters – but with no toilet facilities, customers had to relieve themselves outside or in the Thames!

If you were lucky enough to afford to go to school, you would have had a very early wake-up call, with an average school day starting at seven in the morning! Many children couldn't afford it as they were too poor, so they would have learnt a trade and gone to work or gone begging instead.

# The Prince and the Pauper

For Finn and Elliot
Scarlet and Louie
Mark and Alice

## Acknowledgements

Thank you Purni Morell, Selina Cartmell, Antony Elvin, Kate Waters, Tom Curran, the creative team, all at the Unicorn and Giles Smart.

Thanks are also due to Danielle Bird, Nichole Bird, Nick Boulton, Richard Evans, Jon Glew, Jake Harders, Jason Morell and Kathy Toy for their contributions to both script and music.

The lyrics to songs 'What An England You Must Know', 'So Bittersweet', 'The Royal Admin Song' and 'If I Could Be Queen' were co-written with Antony Elvin.

*The Prince and the Pauper* was first performed at the Unicorn Theatre on 30 November 2012 and featured the following cast and creative team:

| | |
|---|---|
| **Prince Edward, Guildhall Servant** | Danielle Bird |
| **Tom Canty, Prisoner 3** | Nichole Bird |
| **Rich Gentleman, John Canty, Henry VIII, Servant 1, Spanish Ambassador, Judge, Jailer, Tailor** | Nicholas Boulton |
| **Father Andrew, Royal Doctor, Beggar 2, Hobbs, Watchman, Prisoner 4, Archbishop** | Richard Evans |
| **Rent Collector, Beggar 1, Lord Hertford, Sentry Guard, Servant 3, Constable, Sir Hugh, Prisoner 1** | Jonathan Glew |
| **Busker, Servant 2, Miles Hendon, French Ambassador** | Jake Harders |
| **Fine Lady, Bet, Lady Elizabeth, Serving Wench, Reveller, Prisoner 2** | Jason Morell |
| **Ma Canty, Lord Chancellor, Woman with Pig, Lady Edith** | Katherine Toy |

*Director*   Selina Cartmell
*Composer and Music Director*   Antony Elvin
*Set and Projections*   Garance Marneur
*Lighting*   Chahine Yavroyan
*Costumes*   Susan Kulkarni
*Musical Supervisor*   Tom Curran
*Fight / Movement Director*   Kate Waters

## Characters

Tom Canty
Ma Canty
Bet Canty
John Canty
Edward Prince of Wales
King Henry VIII
Lady Elizabeth
Lord Hertford
Lord Chancellor
Miles Hendon
Sir Hugh Hendon
Lady Edith
Busker
Father Andrew
Royal Doctor
Archbishop
Hobbs
Rent Collector
Constable
Woman with Pig
Judge
Royal Tailor
French Ambassador
Spanish Ambassador
Beggar 1
Beggar 2
Servant 1
Servant 2
Servant 3
Reveller
Jailer
Prisoner 1
Prisoner 2
Prisoner 3
Prisoner 4

Sentry Guard
Serving Wench
Watchman
Rich Gentleman
Fine Lady
Guildhall Servant

*The play can be performed with
a minimum of eight actors. For
this size cast doubling is suggested
as follows:*

**1** Tom Canty / Prisoner 3

**2** Prince Edward / Guildhall
Servant

**3** Busker / Miles Hendon /
Servant 2 / French Ambassador

**4** John Canty / Henry VIII /
Servant 1 / Spanish Ambassador /
Judge / Jailer / Tailor / Rich
Gentleman

**5** Mrs Canty / Lord Chancellor /
Woman with Pig / Lady Edith

**6** Lord Hertford / Rent Collector /
Beggar 1 / Sentry Guard /
Servant 3 / Reveller / Constable /
Sir Hugh / Prisoner 1

**7** Bet / Lady Elizabeth / Serving
Wench / Prisoner 2 / Fine Lady

**8** Father Andrew / Royal Doctor /
Beggar 2 / Hobbs / Watchman /
Prisoner 4 / Archbishop

## Prologue

*A troupe of travelling actors enters with a box of costumes. They set the box down and begin to pull out hats, sticks, props. There may be some squabbling over who will wear what. When each actor has found a costume he or she is happy with, they reassemble downstage and ready themselves for the performance of their show.*

**Busker**   We're here to set down a tale as it was told to me by one who had it of his father, who had it of his father, who in like manner had it of *his* father . . . you get the idea anyway. It happened almost five hundred years ago. It may be history. It may be only legend. Oh well. You decide

*Curtains open to reveal a city scene from Tudor England. Members of the troupe play a musical accompaniment, led by the **Busker** on guitar or lute.*

*Act One*

**Scene One**

**Busker**   1546. London town. The richest city in England. Home to kings and queens, knights and merchants, lords and ladies of noble birth.

*A* **Rich Gentleman** *and a* **Fine Lady** *enter. The gentleman bows. She curtseys.*

**Busker**   The majestic River Thames. The glittering palace at Westminster. The ancient Tower of London, which echoes with the THUMP of heads striking the cold stone floor. For King Henry the Eighth likes to set an example by beheading those who break his laws.

**Ma Canty** *enters with a begging bowl.*

**Ma Canty**   Spare a penny, kind sir, help me feed my children. They've had no bread since Sunday.

**Gentleman**   Try earning your bread with an honest day's work.

**Fine Lady**   Don't let her come any closer, sir, she's probably riddled with disease.

**Busker**   1546. London Town. The poorest slum in England. Home to the orphaned, the hungry, the desperate. A city of haves and have-nots. Want and want-nots. Of princes and paupers alike. And yet for all they understand of each other, they may as well live in different countries. Perhaps it's not so different from today.

**Ma Canty** *picks the lady's pocket. The* **Lady** *exits.*

**Busker**
    Offal Court off Pudding Lane
    A London you wouldn't believe

    If your pockets are full when you enter
    They'll be empty when you leave.

**Canty** *enters and whistles at* **Ma**.

**Canty**    Ma Canty! Upstairs, now! The rent collector saw me drinking in the Lamb and Flag. He'll be here any minute to collect his dues.

**Canty** *and* **Ma** *run up a rickety staircase to their hovel as* **Tom** *enters, reading aloud from a book.*

**Tom**    'Should a gentleman be required to approach a royal person, he must doff his hat with the left hand, and bow until his knee touches the ground.'

*The* **Rent Collector** *enters.* **Tom** *practises doffing his hat and bows to him.*

**Tom**    How fare thee, Your Majesty?

**Rent Collector**    Enough of the airs and graces, Tom. Where's your father? He owes me money.

*Tom consults his book but can't find the right response.*

**Tom** (*out*)    It doesn't say anything here about how to approach a rent collector. (*To the* **Rent Collector**.) I'm sure Pa would pay up if he had the money, sir. One day our fortunes will change and then we'll make good your debt.

**Rent Collector**    Dream on, kid. If you're born a pauper, you die a pauper. The sooner you realise that the better.

*He steps aside to let* **Tom** *pass.*

**Busker**
    Offal Court off Pudding Lane
    The home of Tom Canty
    Nine years old and a fine young lad
    Though his father may not agree.

**Tom** *heads home. Upstairs,* **Ma Canty** *and* **Bet** *empty their pockets into* **Canty**'s *hat.*

**Canty**    Is that it? From a whole day's begging?

**Ma Canty**    We did our best, John. People don't have change to spare these days.

**Bet**    They're all flat broke.

**Canty**    I'll break *you* if you don't step up.

*The* **Rent Collector** *bangs on the door.*

**Rent Collector**    John Canty? Open up. If you've money enough to buy ale, you can pay your rent. That's two months you owe me now. (*Beat.*) No? Then I'll be back tomorrow. And this time I'll break the door down.

*He goes downstairs.*

**Ma Canty**    What will we do?

**Canty**    You'll have to beg harder, that's what. (*He grabs* **Bet** *by the hair.*) Or I'll take her to the marketplace and sell her for a slave.

**Bet**    I'll do better, Pa, I promise.

**Tom** (*trying the door*)    Ma? It's me, Tom.

**John Canty** *unlocks the door and pulls* **Tom** *in.*

**Canty**    Where have you been, you lazy mutt? (*He grabs the book.*) And what the devil is this?

**Tom**    It's a book.

**Canty**    I know what a bleeding book is! What's it for?

**Tom**    It's for learning about what life's like in a royal palace. Father Andrew gave it to me. He wants me to be a gentleman and help me improve my mind.

**Canty** *whacks* **Tom**.

**Canty**    Who cares about your filthy mind? You're a pauper. A gutterling. A boil on the bum of humanity. Now turn your pockets out and show me what you got.

**Tom** *does. They're empty.*

**Tom**   None of the merchants gave me a penny today. They're all too worried about King Henry – they say he'll die before the week is out.

**Ma Canty**   And not a moment too soon, that greedy tyrant.

**Canty**   Shut it! (*He collars* **Tom**.) You owe me, boy. Don't I put a roof over your head?

**Tom**   Yes, Pa.

**Canty**   And a crust in your belly?

**Tom**   Yes, Pa.

**Canty**   Then it's time you paid your way. I'm going to the bookseller. This should be worth a few shillings.

**Ma Canty**   You wouldn't be so cruel, John! The tales of palace life give the boy hope.

**Canty**   Hope? A beggar's got no use for hope. It's fear that'll keep him alive, you hear me? Fear!

**All**   Yes, Pa.

**Canty**   Now get out of my way. And lock the door behind me.

*He exits.*

**Ma Canty**   Don't cry, Tom. I'll find you another book some day.

**Tom**   I'm not crying. Just something in my eye . . .

**Bet**   I'm hungry, Ma.

**Ma Canty**   I know, my love. If I thought it would help feed you I'd sell myself in the marketplace.

**Tom**   It's all right, Ma. The book may have gone, but it's given us food and drink already.

**Bet**   Food and drink? Where?

**Tom** (*taps his head*)    In here. Pa was wrong. We beggars need hope more than anyone. Hope and imagination. (*He pulls a crust of bread from his pocket and gives it to* **Bet**.) For the princess. An exotic fruit from the Barbary Coast.

**Bet**    What's fruit?

**Tom**    It's what they eat at court. Won't you taste it, my lady?

**Bet**    It's like . . . sugared almonds from King Henry's own table.

**Tom**    You're getting the hang of it. And can you hear the sweet music from the court musicians?

*Through the window comes a blast of Offal Court: pigs, drunks, beggars, etc.*

**Bet**    I can, my lord. (*Out.*) Sort of.

**Ma Canty**    If I was queen, I'd make sure every orphan in Offal Court got fed.

**Bet**    If I was queen I'd have six meals a day, and furs and gowns galore.

**Tom**    If I was king I'd grant all of your wishes. But first, Your Majesty, pray seat yourself at the royal table and feast to your heart's content.

*He produces another crust for* **Ma Canty**.

**Ma Canty**    I swear you've better manners than the young Prince of Wales himself.

**Tom**    What I'd give for a glimpse of him. Then I'd know how a real prince conducts himself.

**Ma Canty**    Don't you worry, son. I like you just as you are.

*Below in the street the* **Busker** *sings.*

**Busker**
    Offal Court off Pudding Lane
    Where hungry bellies groan
    And boys and girls must beg for bread
    For there's no food at home

Offal Court off Pudding Lane
Where the wind cuts like a knife
Yet half a mile down river
It's a different sort of life.

## Scene Two

*Westminster Palace,* **King Henry***'s chambers.* **Henry** *lies in bed, eating a roast chicken. The royal* **Doctor***,* **Lord Hertford** *and* **Prince Edward** *stand by.*

**Doctor**    On the count of three. One . . . two . . . three . . . heave!

**Lord Hertford** *lifts* **Henry***'s bad leg on to the bed.*

**Henry**    Mind my gammy leg. And pass the salt.

**Hertford**  How are you tonight, Your Majesty?

**Henry**    Sick as a pike.

**Doctor**    Your Majesty, you must eat less, drink less, and take more exercise.

**Henry**    I hate exercise.

**Edward**    But you invented tennis, Father.

**Henry**    Tennis is a passing fad. It will not last. And nor shall I. More wine!

**Doctor**    Is that wise, Your Majesty? Everything in moderation.

**Henry**    You should have told me that before I took six wives. It's a miracle I'm not a raving alcoholic.

*The* **Chancellor** *enters.*

**Henry**    Ah, Lord Chancellor.

**Chancellor**    You called for me, Your Majesty?

**Henry**    Yes. It's time we had a talk about the future of the throne. (*To* **Edward**.) Edward, if I am to die, as the doctor predicts, then you will be king.

**Edward**    Don't say that, Father.

**Henry**    We must face the truth like men, Edward.

**Edward**    But I'm not a man,, Father (*Out.*) I'm only nine.

**Henry**    True say. So we must elect a Lord Protector to look after state affairs until you come of age.

**Chancellor** (*indicating* **Hertford**)    Lord Hertford, Your Majesty, is the natural candidate for Lord Protector.

**Hertford**    I've been your adviser these fifteen years, sire. I hope I've proved both wise and fair.

**Henry**    Fair? What good is fairness in these troublesome times, with the French and the Scots both waiting to invade us? It's brute strength that will protect England, not fairness. Or you'll all be eating snails and wearing skirts before I'm cold in my grave. Mmm, gravy.

**Edward**    But Father, I don't want to learn brute strength. I'd rather study Latin.

**Henry**    Tell me, son. What do you think makes a man a king?

**Edward**    That his father was a king before him?

**Henry**    Yes – but what makes a man a great king?

**Edward**    That he takes good care of his subjects?

**Henry**    Yes – but for what will a great king be most remembered?

**Edward** (*thinks*)    That he invented tennis?

**Henry**    No! A great king must rule his land with absolute authority. That means punishment, not mercy. Discipline, not softness. The stamp of royal authority. (*He holds up the Seal.*) Every king of England inherits the Royal Seal when he is crowned. Use it to seal your letters and decrees, to prove they are by your royal command. Well, boy? Take it. It will be yours soon enough.

**Edward**    But I don't want it, Father. I'm not king yet.

**Henry**    Like it or not, it is your duty. (*He takes* **Edward** *aside.*) You must keep the Seal safe, Edward. Hide it where nobody can find it. If it were to fall into the wrong hands, all manner of ill might happen.

**Edward** (*taking the Seal*)    Very well, Father. But please let's talk no more of death and duty. I'm sure you'll feel better very soon.

**Henry**    You're a good son, Edward. But you have a lot to learn. Tomorrow, you will go to the palace gates and greet your public. They must learn to fear their young prince.

**Edward**    But I'm not as frightening as you, Father. (*Out.*) I'm only nine, remember.

**Henry**    Age has no bearing on leadership. A king needs a steady eye. A firm chin. And a stern countenance.

**Edward**    A steady eye. (*He squints.*) A firm chin. (*He juts out his chin.*) And a stern countenance. (*He tries all three.*) It hurts, Father.

**Henry**    You'll get used to it. Now, off to bed with you. I need my beauty sleep.

*The* **Busker** *enters and sings as the scene changes.*

**Busker**
    The palace at Westminster
    The seat of queens and kings
    Where silver bowls and crystal cups
    Are ordinary things

    The palace at Westminster
    A place of pomp and wealth
    Yet all the gold in Christendom
    Can't buy King Henry's health.

## Scene Three

*The* **Busker** *takes his place on the corner of Offal Court.* **Tom** *and* **Bet** *are begging.*

**Bet**    Spare any change?

**Tom**    Spare any change, sir?

*The* **Rich Gentleman** *enters.*

**Gentleman**    Get a job, you lazy hounds.

**Bet**    There ain't no jobs for the likes of us. Would you rather we picked your pocket?

**Gentleman**    Filthy vermin.

*He spits at them and walks on.*

**Bet**    Bumface!

**Tom**    Hush, Bet. If we must beg for a living, at least let us try to keep good manners.

**Bet**    It's hard to have good manners when the wind's whistling through your drawers.

**Tom**    Just remember what I taught you. Graceful and sweet, like a true princess.

**Bet** *calls to the* **Gentleman**.

**Bet**    (*posh voice*)    Prithee, kind sir, might you spare a penny for our misfortune?

**Gentleman**    Hark. A poor young lady fallen on bad times. Here, my dear.

*He tosses* **Bet** *a coin.*

**Bet**    Thank you, sir! (*To* **Tom**.) Maybe you're right. People ain't so quick to judge when you've got courtly manners.

**Father Andrew** *enters, a ragged priest.*

**Father Andrew**    Afternoon, my children. Are you enjoying your book on life at court, Tom?

**Tom**    Father Andrew, I confess I gave the book to my father so that he might sell it and buy food for the family.

**Bet**    No you didn't! And Pa spent the money on beer!

**Tom**    A prince wouldn't bear a grudge against his father. He'd make the best of it and show forgiveness.

**Father Andrew**    Don't you worry, lad. It was yours to do with as you liked.

**Bet**    So you ain't angry with him?

**Father Andrew**    It's not for me to pass judgment. Leave that to God and King Henry.

**Bet**    What does King Henry care for the likes of us?

**Father Andrew**    Hush, Bet! You must not speak ill of the king.

**Bet**    Why not? Doesn't he sit in the palace stuffing on roasted goose while we're starving in the street?

**Father Andrew**    Try to follow your brother's example, my child. Didn't Tom show forgiveness when your father traded his book for ale?

**Tom**    But how did you –

**Father Andrew**    An educated guess. The man doesn't deserve your loyalty. (*To* **Bet**.) But you see Tom gives it just the same.

*A* **Beggar** *runs on.*

**Beggar 1**    Prince Edward's making a public appearance! The palace gates in half an hour!

**Tom**    The Prince of Wales! Oh, Bet, you know how much I've longed to see him.

**Bet**    I'm not coming. If I see the prince's plump cheeks and fur cloak, I'll only feel my own rags all the worse.

**Tom**    Forget his clothes. Think of his fine manners and princely bearing.

**Bet**    You can copy Prince Edward's bows and flourishes all you like, Tom. You'll never be a prince yourself.

**Tom**    But I can still dream.

*He exits.*

**Bet**    These grand ideas will ruin our Tom.

**Father Andrew**    Who can blame the boy for wanting to better himself? Come, my dear. I'll take you to the church kitchen and find you a morsel to eat.

*They exit.*

**Busker** (*out*)    Who *can* blame Tom, indeed? Or the crowd who followed him through Temple Bar and Charing village and thence to Westminster, all of them hoping for a glimpse of the royal Prince Edward.

## Scene Four

*The **Crowd** pushes towards the gates, guarded by a **Sentry**. **Tom** stands at the back, trying to see through their shoulders.*

**Crowd**
   Where d'you think he is then?
   Is he coming or not?
   I took the morning off for this
   D'you call in sick, or what?
   Look! The doors are opening
   I told them I'd got the plague
   I think that's him approaching
   You dirty lying knave!

*The* **Crowd** *screams with excitement as* **Edward** *approaches. His face is set in the kingly countenance his father showed him.*

**Crowd**
Ooh! Prince Edward
Look at his lovely clothes
Oh! Prince Edward
Look at his lovely nose
Ah, Prince Edward
Blow us a kiss for luck
Wait what's happened to his face?
Looks like something got stuck!

**Tom** *crawls between the legs of the crowd as they surge forwards.*

**Tom**    Help! I can't breathe!

*He uses the* **Sentry Guard**'s *leg to pull himself upright. The* **Guard** *grabs* **Tom** *by the scruff of the neck.*

**Sentry Guard**    You scurvy nipper! You can't use a King's Guard as a stepladder. I'll have you thrown in the Tower.

**Crowd**    Oooh!

**Edward** *approaches the* **Sentry Guard**.

**Edward**    How dare you manhandle the poor lad like that? Put him down.

**Crowd**    Oooh!

*The* **Sentry Guard** *drops* **Tom**.

**Sentry Guard**    Forgive me, Your Highness. I was only trying to protect you.

**Edward**    I need no protection from a beggar boy. Now open the gates and let him in.

**Crowd**    OOOH!

*The gates swing open.* **Tom** *totters towards* **Prince Edward**.

**Edward**    Are you all right, lad? You're as white as a ghost.

**Tom**    Yes, Your Highness. Thank you, Your Highness. I mean to say, Your Highness . . .

*He attempts to doff his hat and make a bow, but faints instead. The* **Crowd** *gasps.*

**Edward**    Take him inside. The poor boy's overcome.

*A* **Servant** *picks up* **Tom** *and carries him away.* **Edward** *follows.*

**Crowd**
    What was that about then
    I can't believe my eyes
    Taking in a beggar boy
    He's in for a surprise
    It's a bit of an anti-climax, eh
    Let's go to the Tower instead
    Yeah all right, if we're lucky
    We'll see somebody lose his head.


**Scene Five**

**Edward***'s chambers. The* **Servant** *enters, carrying* **Tom***.*

**Edward**    Set him down.

**Servant 1**    Is that wise, my lord? He's covered in mud.

**Edward**    A little mud will wash out.

**Servant 1**    Are you sure, my lord? He's probably crawling with lice.

**Edward**    Just do as I say!

*He waves him away with a royal flick. The* **Servant** *puts* **Tom** *down and exits.*

**Edward**    A real pauper. I've never seen one up close before. Ah, he wakes.

**Tom** (*eyes still shut*)    Oh, Ma, what I dream I had. I met the Prince of Wales at Westminster Palace, and I don't know which was the handsomer.

**Edward**    A pretty way you have with words, for a beggar boy. What is your name?

**Tom** *jumps up.*

**Tom**    Tom Canty, Your Highness.

**Edward**    And where do you live?

**Tom**    Offal Court, Your Highness.

**Edward**    Awful Court? It sounds most grim. And have you a mother and father?

**Tom**    Yes, Your Highness, and a sister, Bet.

*He makes a graceful bow to the* **Prince**.

**Edward**    I have a sister too, the Lady Elizabeth. In faith, your manners are not those of a pauper boy.

**Tom**    I've had schooling from Father Andrew, Your Highness, and I taught myself manners from books. But I never thought to step inside a real palace.

**Edward**    And how do you find it?

**Tom**    Exquisite, Your Highness.

**Edward**    Well, Tom Canty, but for your rags and mud, nobody in court should ever take you for a beggar boy. You must be hungry, lad. (*He offers* **Tom** *a bowl of fruit.*) Help yourself while we wait for supper.

**Tom**    What is it?

**Edward**    Why, it's fruit.

**Tom**    So *this* is fruit. I read of it in my book.

**Edward**    You mean you've never eaten a pear or an apple? Then, truly, your life is poor and mean.

**Tom** *eats a pear, closes his eyes in ecstasy.*

**Tom**   It doesn't seem so mean just now. I've never tasted such ripeness.

**Edward**   Talking of ripeness . . . (*He sniffs* **Tom**.) You smell as though you haven't bathed for a week.

*He spritzes* **Tom** *with perfume.*

**Tom** (*out*)   It was actually last spring.

**Edward**   That's better. The only thing left of Awful Court is your awful pauper's rags. With a good suit of clothes, I swear none in the palace would ever guess you weren't a prince yourself.

**Tom**   Oh, to be dressed just once in fine attire. I've dreamed of how it would feel.

**Edward**   Then you shall.

**Tom**   Very well, Your Highness.

*They exchange clothes.*

*Song: 'What an England You Must Know'.*

**Tom**
Oh, Your Highness, how rich these clothes do feel
As soft as fur and warm as sun, it doesn't quite seem real
How wonderful your life must be, you've never felt a blow
Just honour and decorum –

**Tom / Edward**
What an England you must know

**Edward**
How light and free these rags feel
With no buttons and no pins
How light and free your life must be
With no pressure from the king
No palace guards or servants a-rushing to and fro
Just liberty and laughter –

**Tom / Edward**
What an England you must know

**Edward** *leads* **Tom** *to a looking glass.*

**Edward**
By God, just look at us
Same hair, same face, same eyes

**Tom / Edward**
Same gait, same weight, same height
The ultimate disguise

**Edward**
Two peas in a pod

**Tom**
Two dice in a cup

**Tom / Edward**
Two toads in the hole

**Edward**
No buttons and no pins

**Tom**
Honour and decorum
To never feel a blow

**Edward**
Oh Tom Canty, such freedoms I'll never know

**Tom**
No Your Highness, you really don't want to know

**Edward**
To walk the streets of London

**Tom**
To feel this royal glow

**Tom / Edward**
Perhaps we're not so different
What an England you must know
What an England we must know.

**Tom** *fishes in his pocket in the Prince's clothes and removes the Royal Seal.*

**Tom**    Is this yours, Your Highness? It's very pretty. What is it?

**Edward** *snatches the Seal from* **Tom**.

**Edward**    Why, it's a – a nutcracker. Now close your eyes, boy, just for a second.

**Tom**    Of course, Your Highness.

*He hides his face while* **Edward** *hides the Seal in a suit of armour.*

**Edward** (*out*)    Thank goodness he found the Royal Seal. Imagine my father's anger if I'd lost it! (*To* **Tom**.) Ready, lad.

**Tom**    Oh. You didn't hide.

*A new* **Servant** *enters with food.*

**Edward**    No matter. Supper is arrived. (*To the* **Servant**.) Set it down and then leave us.

*The* **Servant** *ignores* **Edward** *and addresses* **Tom**.

**Servant 2**    What is your wish, Your Highness?

**Tom**    Eh?

**Edward**    He's mistaken us. Pretend you're me and command him.

**Tom** (*to the* **Servant**, *in princely voice*)    Set it down and leave us. The pauper and I have business to attend to.

**Servant 2**    Very good, Your Highness.

**Edward** (*to the* **Servant**, *in pauper voice*)    Oi mate, bung us a chicken wing, I'm famished.

*The* **Servant** *exits.* **Tom** *and* **Edward** *laugh.*

**Edward**    I swear, I've not had this much fun since my father's jester fell downstairs and broke his neck. If Papa wasn't so ill, I'd take you to his chamber right now and see if we could fool him too.

**Tom**    Oh no, Your Highness. King Henry might not get the joke and throw me in the Tower.

**Edward**    Why is everyone so scared of my father? He's perfectly nice when you get to know him.

*The* **Chancellor** *enters, bows to* **Tom**.

**Chancellor** (*to* **Tom**)    My lord, your father bids you come to his chamber.

**Tom** (*as himself*)    My father? He's usually in the Lamb and Flag this time of day.

**Chancellor**    Your grace, this is no time for jest. Come along at once.

**Edward**    You have things backwards, Lord Chancellor. I'm the prince, not he.

**Chancellor**    I beg your pardon?

**Edward**    It is granted. (*To* **Tom**.) We'll have to continue another time. Give me my clothes and be on your way, lad.

*He moves towards* **Tom**, *but the* **Chancellor** *steps between them.*

**Chancellor**    How dare you approach the Prince of Wales, you yeasty little hedgepig! Servant!

**Servant 1** *re-enters.*

**Chancellor**    Take this beggar back to the street where he belongs.

**Servant 1** *picks* **Edward** *up and puts him over his shoulder.*

**Edward**    Put me down! You've got the wrong boy.

**Tom**    It's no lie, sire. I'm the pauper, he's His Royal Highness the Prince of Wales!

**Chancellor** (*to* **Tom**) Please, your grace, that's quite enough of this foolishness! (*To the* **Servant**.) Take him away.

**Edward**    Put me down, I tell you! Stop them, Tom! Tom?

**Tom** *runs after* **Edward**, *but the* **Chancellor** *stops him.*
**Edward** *and the* **Servant** *exit.*

**Tom**    Please my lord, it was just a game. I didn't mean no harm.

**Chancellor**    You must prepare for the worst, Your Highness. Before the day is out you might be king of England.

**Tom**    But that's impossible. I'm only Tom Canty from Offal Court.

**Chancellor**    Really, sire. Your father warned you about reading too many books.

**Tom** (*weeping*)    He did, my lord, and he beat me for it. (*Out.*) But I'd give anything to have Pa here now to prove I'm telling the truth.


**Scene Six**

*Palace gates. The* **Sentry Guard** *still stands on duty.*

**Busker**
    O Prince Edward
    Tudor son
    Born in the royal palace
    O Prince Edward
    Chosen one
    Bred in the royal palace
    O Prince Edward
    Fair of face
    Loved by all the populace
    O Prince Edward
    Young Prince Edward
    Son of the royal palace.

*The* **Servant** *frogmarches* **Edward** *through the gates, throws him down, then exits.*

**Edward**    Blaggard! Scoundrel! Knave!

*A* **Crowd** *gathers to watch.*

**Sentry Guard**    Well, well, if it isn't the little pauper what got me in trouble with the prince. Had enough of you, has he?

**Edward**    I'm no pauper. I'm the Prince of Wales!

*Everybody roars with laughter.*

**Sentry Guard**    Yeah, yeah, and I'm the Sultan of Persia.

**Edward**    It's *true*. In the name of God, man, don't you recognise me either?

**Sentry Guard**    I recognise your rags. And your ratty little face. And the stink on you. Now get away from the palace gates before I have you thrown in jail.

**Edward**    You will pay for this, you mark my words. (*To the* **Crowd**.) Someone tell me where might I find Awful Court where the Canty family lives. They're my only hope to prove I am who I say.

**Crowd 1**    Then I wish you luck, mate. A meaner drunk than John Canty never breathed the air.

**Edward**    If you know him, take me to him.

**Crowd**    What's it worth?

**Edward**    I have no money to pay you now, but I shall just as soon as I'm back in the palace –

**Crowd 2**    Think we were born yesterday, mate?

**Crowd 3**    Show us the cash and we'll be yer guide. Without it you're on yer own.

**Edward** *turns out his pockets – they're empty. The* **Crowd** *laughs.*

**Crowd 1**    See you, Yer Highness.

**Crowd 2**    Don't get lost, Yer Highness

**Crowd 3**    And watch out for that John Canty. His bite's even worse than his bark.

*They sing to* **Edward** *mockingly as he walks away.*

**Crowd**
> Make way for the Prince of Poverty
> Make way for the Monarch of Mud
> Make way for his Royal Raggedness
> There's no blue in his blood
> Make way for the Lord of the Loafers
> Make way for Sir Stumblebum
> Make way for the Duke of Down-and-Outs
> The lying pauper scum
> The lying pauper scum!

**Edward** (*out*)   If I'm to be on my own, then I must make do with what I have. A steady eye. (*He squints.*) A firm chin. (*He juts out his chin.*) And a stern countenance.

**Edward** *sets off along the river.*

**Busker**
> Poor Prince Edward
> Tudor son
> Bred in the royal palace
> Poor Prince Edward
> On the run
> Kicked out of the royal palace
> Poor Prince Edward
> All alone
> Swapped his riches for rags and bones
> Poor Prince Edward
> Brave Prince Edward
> Far from the royal palace.

**Scene Seven**

**Tom** *stands alone, quaking.* **King Henry** *enters with the* **Doctor**, *the* **Chancellor** *and* **Lord Hertford**.

**Henry**   Well, Edward. Is it true you disobeyed me this morning?

**Tom**    Your M-M-M-M-Majesty . . . ?

**Henry**    I asked you to greet your public at the palace gates, but I hear you were there but a minute before you went back inside to play.

**Tom**    But p-p-p-p-please, Your M-M-M-Majesty . . .

**Henry**    What ails you, boy? Speak up!

*The* **Doctor**, **Hertford** *and the* **Chancellor** *peer at* **Tom**. *He bursts into tears.*

**Tom**    I want my m-m-m-m –

**Doctor**    Medicine?

**Tom**    No, my m-m-m-m –

**Hertford**    Midday meal?

**Tom**    No, my m-m-m-m –

**Chancellor**    Mary Queen of Scots, your second cousin once removed?

**Tom**    My m-m-m-m-muvver!

**Henry**    Muvver? Your *mother's* been dead these nine years, son.

**Doctor**    I fear the prince is unwell, sire. See how he shakes.

**Chancellor**    Perhaps the beggar I found in his chambers has infected him with a disease.

**Henry**    Well, I won't stand for it. (*To* **Tom**.) You're a royal prince, not a little girl. Pull yourself together!

**Tom** *sobs, terrified.*

**Hertford**    The doctor should examine him, sire. He's not himself at all.

**Henry**    This is all I ruddy need. Tomorrow is the banquet for the foreign ambassadors. Edward must attend in my place. I feel my end is near. (*A fart.*)

**Chancellor**    It certainly is.

*The* **Doctor** *looks in* **Tom**'*s ears and mouth, taps his head, tests his reflexes.*

**Doctor**   Prince Edward, what are seven times seven?

**Tom**   Forty-nine, sir.

**Doctor**   He hasn't forgotten his arithmetic. (*To* **Tom**.) *Quid agis?*

**Tom**   *Bene, et tu?*

**Doctor**   Nor his Latin, either. (*To* **Tom**.) And now, pray, tell us your name?

**Tom**   Tom Canty, sir.

**Henry**   Well, doctor, what is your diagnosis?

**Doctor**   Mad as a box of frogs.

**Henry**   This is grievous news.

**Hertford**   Indeed, my lord. But we must act as if nothing is wrong. Ill or not, Prince Edward should attend the Ambassadors' banquet, or gossip and rumour will abound.

**Henry**   Very well. Any man who speaks of my son's malady shall pay for it with his life. We must show the people that you cannot trifle with a Tudor! Oooh, trifle. (*To* **Tom**.) Edward, I asked you yesterday what makes a king great. Well?

**Tom** (*thinks*)   Is it that he invented tennis, Your Majesty?

**Henry**   No! A great king must show strength. Not weakness of mind or heart. You must drop this make-believe at once.

**Tom**   But, it isn't make-believe, Your M-M-M-Majesty –

**Henry**   Promise me, son, or you'll face my anger from beyond the grave.

**Tom**   I promise, your M-M-M-Majesty.

**Henry**   Now let me finish my supper. All this trouble has made me hungry.

**Tom** (*to* **Hertford**)    I'm not going home to Offal Court, am I?

**Hertford**    No, my liege. You are a prince, not a pauper. And before too long the whole of England will be in your hands.

**Tom** *looks at his hands, then the audience.*

**Tom** (*out*)    Oh *g-g-g-g-gawd.*

**Busker**
Poor Tom Canty
No more fun
Here in the royal palace
Poor Tom Canty
Henry's son
Trapped in the royal palace
Oh Tom Canty
Prince at last
But his hopes are fading fast
Poor Tom Canty
Scared Tom Canty
Trapped in the royal palace.


**Scene Eight**

*Offal Court.* **Edward** *enters. He stops a* **Beggar***.*

**Edward**    Where might I find the Canty dwelling?

**Beggar 2**    Canty? That's their hovel up there.

**Edward**    There? No wonder the lad looked so ill.

**Beggar 2**    At least they've got a roof over their heads.

**Edward**    A roof that leaks, surely?

**Beggar 2**    I'd give me right arm for a roof that leaks.

**Beggar 1**    You ain't got a right arm – the plague took it.

**Beggar 2**    All right, I'd give me left toe for a roof that leaks.

**Beggar 1**   You ain't got a left toe either.

**Beggar 2**   Whatever.

**Bet** *enters.*

**Bet**   Tom! (*She gives him a kiss.*) I was worried about you.
You've been gone for hours.

**Edward**   Urgh. Get off me, girl.

**Bet**   What's wrong with you? Didn't you catch a look at the
prince after all?

**Edward**   I *am* the prince. Are you Tom Canty's sister Bet?

**Bet**   What's this new game? (*She mock-curtseys.*) Why yes, Your
Royal Highness.

**Edward**   That's better. Now, prithee, where are your
parents? I must speak to them at once about your brother Tom.

**Bet** (*playing along*)   Why, what's he done now?

**Edward**   He's sitting in my royal chamber dressed in my
clothes, that's what.

**Bet**   Ooh, lucky Tom.

**Edward**   It was a good joke at first, I admit, but it's not
funny any more. I've missed my supper and these rags of his
let in the cold.

**Bet**   Best take you home then, and give you a new suit and
a hot dinner.

*She links arms with* **Edward** *and tries to drag him off.*

**Edward**   Let go of me, you mannerless wench! I could have
you put in the stocks for less.

**Bet**   And I could put you over my knee. You may be good at
make-believe, but you're still my little brother.

**Canty** *reels on, drunk, holding a bottle of beer.*

**Bet**    Look, here's Pa. And he's drunk as a lord. You'd better drop your act, Tom, you know it makes him mad.

**Edward**    That's your father there? That ruffian?

**Bet**    Sshhh. Evening, Pa.

**Canty**    Same to you. Upstairs, Bet, and get my supper ready.

**Bet**    Yes, Pa.

**Bet** *runs upstairs to the* **Canty** *rooms.* **Canty** *lurches towards* **Edward**.

**Canty**    Well, pizzle face? Where you been all day?

**Edward**    I can tell where *you've* been all day – the ale on your breath could stun a horse!

**Canty**    You cheeky cur!

*He collars* **Edward**.

**Edward**    Ow! Let go of me.

**Canty**    'Let go of me.' You mincing little weasel.

*He wallops* **Edward**.

**Edward**    That hurt, you brute.

**Canty**    It was supposed to hurt. That'll teach you to mock your father.

**Edward**    You are not my father. My father has never struck me before.

**Canty**    Never struck you before? You've got a short memory. Now turn out your pockets.

**Edward**    I'm not taking orders from you, villain.

**Canty**    You what?

*He takes out his cudgel.* **Edward** *tries to hide.*

**Edward**    Would you bruise the tender skin of the future king of England?

*Canty chases* **Edward**.

**Canty**   You what?

**Edward**   Your son Tom Canty and I swapped places for a lark. Now he is in the royal palace mistaken as me, and I am mistaken as him.

**Canty**   You *what*?

*He gets* **Edward** *by the scruff of the neck.*

**Edward**   I'm trying to tell you! I am Edward, Prince of Wales.

**Canty**   Edward Prince of Wales? He's finally lost his marbles. That's all I bleeding need. I'm taking you home before you embarrass me any more.

*He drags* **Edward** *up the stairs.*

**Edward**   Put me down, I tell you!

**Canty**   Cork it!

**Edward**   I take orders from nobody but my father.

**Canty**   Just what I said! CORK IT!

*He plugs* **Edward**'s *mouth with a cork from his bottle of ale. They enter the house.*

**Ma Canty**   Tom, love? There's something wrong with him, John.

**Canty**   You can say that again.

**Ma Canty** (*obediently*)   Tom, love? There's something wrong with him, John.

**Canty**   Shut it, woman! Your son's gone mad. It's your fault for letting him read all them books.

*He throws* **Edward** *down.*

**Ma Canty**   What d'you mean? Are you sick, son?

**Ma** *and* **Bet** *pick* **Edward** *up and uncork him with a pop.*

**Edward**    I'm sick in heart and body, madam, thanks to your villainous husband.

**Canty**    Do you not hear the little upstart? He's Tom no longer, he says he's Edward Prince of Wales.

**Ma Canty**    Oh, Tom lad, those stories have cooked your brain.

**Edward**    Madam, listen to me. Your son Tom is alive and well. If you'll just get me home, my father the king will restore him to you.

**Bet**    Your father the king? That's a joke.

**Canty** *takes a swipe at* **Bet***, misses and stumbles.*

**Canty**    I'm *your* king, you cheeky wench. And where's my bleeding supper?

**Ma Canty** *gives* **Canty** *a piece of bread and takes his beer away.*

**Ma Canty**    Here, John. Now why not lie down and sleep it off?

**Canty**    Cos I'm not tired! (*He eats the bread, yawns, burps.*)

**Ma Canty**    That's right, John, you rest your weary head. (*She leads him to the bed.*) Tom will be right in the morning, you'll see.

**Canty**    He'd better be . . . he's got work to do!

*He falls instantly asleep and starts snoring. Everyone sighs with relief.*

**Edward**    You did well, madam. I feared I was in for another beating.

**Ma Canty**    Tom, don't break my heart. Do you really not know us, your family who loves you?

**Bet**    It's seeing that prince at the palace, ain't it? That's what turned your head?

**Edward**    For the last time, I *am* the prince! (*Tearful.*) And I want my p-p-p-p –

**Ma Canty**    Pudding?

**Edward**   No, my p-p-p-p –

**Bet**   Parrot?

**Edward**   No, my papa, King Henry the Eighth. I'm afraid he'll die before I get home.

**Bet / Ma Canty**   Aaaah, poor little Tom . . .

**Bet**   Witless or not, we still love you.

**Ma Canty**   Your father won't die, love, he's just sleeping like a pig. Now dry your eyes.

*She gives him a handful of straw.* **Edward** *takes it, astonished.*

**Edward**   Am I a horse, madam?

**Ma Canty**   No, lad, you're my own bonny little pony and I won't let you come to no harm. Sleep now . . . you'll feel better on the morrow.

*They wrap* **Edward** *in a ragged blanket and put him to bed.*

**Edward**   I must admit, I'm very tired. (*Yawning.*) Will you promise to take me to the palace first thing?

**Ma Canty**   Of course we will, pet. (*To* **Bet**.) Best humour his fancy, to keep him calm.

*She sings to him as* **Edward** *falls asleep in* **Bet**'s *arms.*

*Song: 'So Bittersweet'.*

**Ma Canty**
　　You, you spent another day on the cold London streets
　　You trudged all the way out west to see real royalty
　　Westminster Hall has given you something brighter
　　Something splendid, something grand
　　Now sleep Your Highness please
　　Dreams are so fleet, so bittersweet.

**Scene Nine**

*The Prince's chambers.* **Tom** *sits in a chair, still dressed in his finery. The table is laid for dinner. Three* **Servants** *stand in attendance.*

**Servant 3**    Are you not hungry, Your Highness?

**Tom**    I am.

**Servant 1**    Would you not eat, Your Highness?

**Tom**    I would. Don't you want to sit down and join me?

*The* **Servants** *titter.*

**Servant 2**    My lord, we are here to *serve* you.

**Servant 3**    You are the prince, my lord, and we are your *servants*.

**Servant 1**    The rumours are true. The poor prince has forgotten all his manners.

**Tom** *examines the knives and forks, and giving up, eats with his fingers.*

**Tom** *(out)*    I never knew being a prince would be such hard work.

**Lady Elizabeth** *enters.*

**Elizabeth**    Well, Edward? Is it true you've gone mad? I hear it amuses you to pretend you're a beggar boy.

**Tom**    Are you the prince's sister, Lady Elizabeth?

**Elizabeth**    No, I'm the Queen of Sheba.

**Tom** *makes a courtly bow.*

**Tom**    Then I'm honoured to make your acquaintance, Your Majesty.

**Elizabeth**    I was joking, stupid. Have you lost your sense of humour as well as your wits?

**Tom**    Lord Hertford says my mind needs a rest, Lady Elizabeth, but that isn't the problem.

**Elizabeth**    What is it, then?

**Tom** (*whispers*)    I'm not a prince at all. I'm Tom Canty, a pauper boy from Offal Court.

**Elizabeth** (*out*)    Mad as a bald peacock. (*To* **Tom**.) If your head is truly gone bad, perhaps we should just chop it off.

**Tom** *falls to his knees.*

**Tom**    Oh, please, my lady – don't put me in the Tower.

**Elizabeth**    It's a game, Edward! I'm practising in case I ever become queen.

**Servants** (*out*)    Thank God that'll never happen.

**Elizabeth**    But you can't go around impersonating a pauper, Edward. The court will never stand for it, and nor will Father. Let me speak with you alone.

*She dismisses the* **Servants** *with an imperious gesture. They back out of the room, bowing as they go.*

**Tom**    How did you do that?

**Elizabeth**    What?

**Tom**    That. (*He copies her gesture.*) I wish I could learn it.

**Elizabeth**    Then I shall teach you whatever your madness has caused you to forget.

**Tom**    Will you, my lady? Lord Hertford tells me I must attend a banquet tomorrow.

**Elizabeth**    First things first, then. The royal flick, when you wish to dismiss your servants.

*She makes the imperious gesture again.* **Tom** *copies it.*

**Elizabeth**    If you want to bid them come closer, the state summons. (*She demonstrates.*) And if they're not in the room, you call for them in a ladylike fashion. SERVICE!

*The three* **Servants** *enter in a hurry.*

**Elizabeth**    Now you try, Edward. Send them away.

**Tom** *tries the royal flick. The* **Servants** *back away obsequiously.*
**Tom** *summons them – they come back.* **Servant 1** *now carries a fruit bowl containing a pineapple.*

**Tom**    I think I've got it.

**Elizabeth**    Jolly good.

**Tom** *takes the pineapple out of the fruit bowl.*

**Tom**    What is *that*?

**Servant 2**    A pine apple, my lord, from the New World. A most barbarous and exotic fruit.

**Tom**    You mean it's to be *eaten*?

**Elizabeth**    It's far too valuable to eat. Father has considerable debts and we've been told we must draw in the royal purse strings, remember?

**Tom**    But then what's the pine apple for?

**Servant 1**    It's been hired for decoration, sire, for the Ambassadors' visit.

**Elizabeth**    Enough! It's impolite to discuss court matters in front of the staff. (*She dismisses the* **Servants** *with the royal flick.*) Forget the lesson, let's play beheadings instead. You be the prisoner and I'll be the executioner.

**Tom**    Can't you pretend you're king instead, and show me mercy?

**Elizabeth** (*out*)    He's even worse than I thought. (*To* **Tom**.) A king doesn't show mercy, Edward, it's simply not the fashion. You'd better go to bed and rest. You've plenty more to learn before the banquet. (*Out.*) At this rate it'll be a right royal embarrassment.

*The* **Busker** *enters and sings as the scene changes to Offal Court.*

**Busker**

O Tom Canty
Pauper son
Prince to all of London
O Tom Canty
Life's begun
As prince to all of London
O Tom Canty
Quite the toff
Wonder if he'll pull it off.

*In Offal Court,* **Ma Canty** *leans out of the window.*

**Ma Canty**    Put a sock in it, mate.

*The* **Busker** *ignores her.*

**Busker**

O Tom Canty
Lucky Tom Canty
Prince to all of London . . .

**Ma Canty** *throws a bucket of water over the* **Busker**'s *head.*

**Busker**    Bleeding peasants.


**Scene Ten**

*The* **Canty** *house. A cock crows. Prince* **Edward** *is in bed,
sandwiched in between* **Bet** *and* **Ma Canty**. **Edward** *stirs and
stretches.*

**Edward**    Oh, Elizabeth, what a strange dream I had. I was
changed to a pauper and trapped in a filthy slum. (*He wakes up.*)
Oh no! Awful Court!

*The* **Rent Collector** *hammers at the door, waking everyone else up.*
**John Canty** *springs to his feet and gestures to everyone to keep quiet.*

**Rent Collector** (*off*)    John Canty? I'm here for my rent. I know you're in there. If you don't open up I'll break this door down.

**Canty**    Make a run for it through the back and down the stairs.

**Ma Canty** *and* **Bet** *exit.* **Canty** *grabs* **Edward**.

**Canty**    Not so fast, my boy. You're coming with me.

**Edward**    But I need to get back to the palace!

**Canty**    Give it a rest, or I'll whip you till your back runs red!

**Rent Collector**    I'm coming in. One. Two. THREE!

*He takes a run at the door, which* **Canty** *opens at the last moment. The* **Rent Collector** *sails through at great speed and lands in the corner.* **Canty** *knifes him dead.*

**Canty**    Bull's eye! Let's scarper.

**Edward**    You murdering scoundrel!

**Canty**    Ah, so what? He was a rent collector. I've done the world a favour.

**Edward**    When I get home, I'll make sure you swing for this, John Canty.

**Canty**    And if you don't shut it, I'll swing for you!

*He drags* **Edward** *downstairs and into Offal Court. A crowd of* **Revellers** *appears.*

**Edward**    Somebody help! This villain's just killed a m –

**Canty** *claps his hand over* **Edward**'s *mouth.*

**Canty**    Mouse. Well, can you blame me, filthy little vermin? What's all the excitement about?

**Reveller**    Young Prince Edward's being feasted at Guildhall. He's taking the Royal Barge along the Thames.

**Edward** *bites* **Canty**'s *hand.* **Canty** *yells out and lets go of him.*

**Edward**   Prince Edward? Being feasted?

**Reveller**   Aye, King Henry's ailing fast. It won't be long before Edward's on the throne.

**Edward**   That swine Tom Canty's pretending to be me! He'll swing alongside his father.

**Canty** *covers* **Edward***'s mouth again.*

**Canty**   Excuse my son, he's soft in the head.

**Edward** *bites him again.* **Canty** *yells with pain.*

**Canty**   Ow! But very sharp of tooth!

**Edward**   I tell you, I've been kidnapped. I'm the real Prince Edward.

*The* **Revellers** *laugh.*

**Canty**   You see? The poor lad's cuckoo. That's why I'm taking him away for a nice long rest in the country.

**Edward** *knees* **Canty** *in the nuts.* **Canty** *lets go.*

**Edward**   And let that beggar boy steal my place? Not likely!

*He dives between the legs of the* **Crowd** *and runs away.* **Canty** *follows.*

**Canty**   Oi, you little bleeder! Come back here!

*He chases* **Edward** *through the streets, weaving in and out of the* **Revellers***, who sing as they make their way to the Thames.* **Edward** *shouts back to them as he runs.*

*Song: 'Let's Go Down the River'.*

**Crowd**
   Let's go down the river, see the prince

**Edward**
   I'm the prince!

**Crowd**
   Let's go down the river catch a glimpse

**Edward**
  I'm the Prince!

**Crowd**
  Let's go down the river
  To see the royal son

**Edward**
  The royal son is on the streets!

**Canty**
  And here his father comes!

**Crowd**
  Let's go down the river, see the prince

**Canty** *gains ground on* **Edward***.*

**Crowd**
  Let's go down and cheer the royal lad

**Edward**
  Are you mad?

**Crowd**
  Let's go down and wave an English flag

**Edward**
  This is bad!

**Crowd**
  Let's go down the river
  And pay him our respects

**Edward**
  The royal lad's in trouble!

**Canty**
  I'll break his bleeding neck!

**Canty** *backs* **Edward** *into a corner. He raises his cudgel.*

**Canty**    You'll defy me no more. I'll pound your bones to pudding, boy.

**Miles Hendon**, *a nobleman dressed in a ragged cloak, steps out of the shadows.*

**Miles**   Those are harsh words for such a young lad.

**Canty**   Who the hell are you?

**Miles**   I am Miles Hendon, soldier by trade, gentleman by nature. And I don't like to see a child mistreated.

**Canty**   Well, I'm his father, and how he's treated is up to me.

**Edward**   It's a lie. He's no kin of mine, in the name of my own father King Henry.

**Canty**   The boy's witless, can't you tell? Now leave us be.

**Miles**   Whether his head is sound or cracked, he's old enough to know his heart. (*To* **Edward**.) Are you in trouble, lad? Do you need help?

**Edward**   Yes, please!

**Miles**   Shall I take you away to a place of safety?

**Edward**   Yes, please!

**Miles**   Then the matter is settled.

**Canty** *pulls out his cudgel.*

**Canty**   Stop right there, or I'll kill the boy right in front of you.

**Miles** *draws his sword expertly.*

**Miles**   Go ahead, punk. *Facete ut gaudeam.*

**Canty**   Eh?

**Miles**   No Latin? Then let's talk a language you'll understand. Lay a finger on him and I'll cut it off, you animated offal.

*The men square up to each other.*

**Canty**   You and whose army, you jumped-up clotpole?

**Miles**    Back off, you beef-witted mammet.

**Canty**    Go to hell, you crusty scullion.

**Miles**    Milk-livered dog-heart!

**Canty**    Mangled clack-dish!

**Miles**    Tottering turd-head!

**Canty**    Spleeny spatch-cock!

**Miles** *backs* **Canty** *up against the wall.*

**Miles**    Lumpish tickle-brained full-gorged mewling pox-marked pignut!

**Canty**    Whatever. You ain't seen the last of me. (*To* **Edward**.) Beware you, boy. You'll regret the day you was ever born.

*He exits.*

**Edward**    Thank you, sire. I feared I'd met my end.

**Miles**    My pleasure. You certainly don't seem half-witted, like that villain said. Now why don't you tell me your name?

**Edward**    My name, good man, is Edward Prince of Wales.

**Miles** (*out*)    I spoke too soon. He's mad as a bag of weasels. (*Slowly, with exaggerated gestures.*) You, lad, come with me. Miles's lodgings. Eat, bathe and rest.

**Edward** (*out*)    After all that, the poor man's a simpleton. Ah well. Beggars can't be choosers.

## Scene Eleven

*Palace.* **Henry**'s *chambers.* **Henry** *is close to death.* **Tom** *stands at the bedside with* **Hertford**.

**Henry**    Well, Lord Hertford, will you stand by my son when I am gone?

**Hertford**    I will, my lord.

**Henry**    Teach him to fight our enemies tooth and nail and show no mercy?

**Hertford**    I will, my lord.

**Henry**    Then I appoint you Lord Protector of the Realm.

**Hertford**    Thank you, my lord.

*He bows to* **Tom** *and exits.* **Henry** *draws* **Tom** *closer.*

**Henry**    Edward, the time has come. I am going . . .

**Tom**    Going?

**Henry**    Going . . .

**Tom**    Going?

**Henry** *falls back on the pillows.* **Tom** *crosses himself.*

**Tom**    Gone.

**Henry**    Don't rush me, son. I haven't had my pudding yet. I have summoned you here to say goodbye. But before I die I must ensure you have made safe with the Royal Seal.

**Tom**    But you can't die, Your Majesty. That would mean . . . (*Working it out.*) It would mean . . .

**Henry**    You will be king, my boy.

**Tom**    But I can't, Your Majesty. It's not possible.

**Henry**    Who else should take the throne then? Not your sister Elizabeth. And certainly not Mary, your second cousin twice removed. She's a Scot.

**Tom**    What?

**Henry**    Exactly. No, Edward, it is your duty to reign over the English people.

**Tom**    Perhaps you'll get better, Your Majesty. (*He brings* **Henry** *the fruit bowl.*) Here, have some fruit. They say it does wonders for the health.

**Henry**   I did fancy to taste a pine apple once more before I die.

**Tom**   Can you afford it, Your Majesty?

**Henry**   I see your wits have not left you entirely. That is good news. But there is no hope for me now. The future of the kingdom lies with you, my boy.

**Elizabeth** *enters and curtseys.*

**Elizabeth**   Hello, Father. You're still alive, then.

**Henry**   Are you in a rush to see me die, Elizabeth?

**Elizabeth**   Of course not, Father. It's just that I'm promised a new gown for Edward's coronation, and I *am* rather looking forward to it.

**Henry** (*out*)   Thank God she'll never be queen.

**Elizabeth**   Come along, Edward. The Royal Barge is waiting to take us to the Guildhall banquet.

**Henry**   Go then, son. Take care of your sister. And don't forget your promises. Guard the Seal. And rule with a fist of iron when I am gone.

**Tom**   I will, Your Majesty. (*Out.*) I know it's a sin to tell a lie. But what would *you* do when the dread King Henry gives you an order? I'm only a pauper, after all. Aren't I?

**Scene Twelve**

**Miles** *tends to* **Edward** *in his lodgings.*

**Miles**   Come, lad. Why don't you rest while we wait for luncheon?

**Edward**   But there's no time. I have to get back to the palace and restore my rightful place.

**Miles** (*out*)    Still he persists with his fantasy. (*To* **Edward**.) Then let's get you out of your beggar's rags.

**Edward**    I may look like a beggar boy, but there's more to me than meets the eye.

**Miles**    *Fructu non folis arborem aestima.*

**Edward**    Judge a tree by its fruit, not its leaves.

**Miles**    You speak Latin?

**Edward**    Of course. And Greek.

**Miles**    Where in heaven did you learn it?

**Edward**    With my private tutor. Do you think the Prince of Wales would be uneducated?

**Miles** (*out*)    It must be a fever of the brain, poor lad. (*To* **Edward**.) Of course not, sire. But I'd think a prince would be clean, at least.

**Miles** *leads* **Edward** *to the washstand and sits down while he washes*

**Edward**    What's this! Would you sit in the presence of a prince?

**Miles** *jumps to his feet, and bows.*

**Miles**    Forgive me, sire, for I've spent these last seven years in a foreign dungeon where manners don't cut much ice.

*A* **Serving Wench** *enters with food and puts it down.*

**Wench**    Here's yer bread and meat. Who's the pauper?

**Edward**    You foul-mannered trollop. Curtsey before your prince.

**Wench**    A prince, is it? That's a coincidence, cos I'm Queen Cleopatra.

**Miles**    Forget her, Your Highness, and eat your fill. (*He takes the* **Wench** *aside.*) He's lost his mind, my dear. The only cure is to play along until he comes to his senses again.

**Wench**   I'll cure the little varmint with the back of my hand.

**Miles**   Come now. Show some charity. Here's a shilling to help you along.

*He gives her a coin and a pat on the bottom.*

**Wench**   Don't take the Michelangelo.

*She exits.*

**Miles**   Eat your fill, lad. We'll have a long journey ahead of us later.

**Edward**   So you'll take me home?

**Miles**   I will, lad, but to *my* home. Hendon Hall. When I left to fight the Turks my brother Hugh was put in charge, but now I'm back to resume my place. Forget your family, and come along with me.

**Edward**   I cannot. My father will be mad with worry.

**Miles** (*out*)   His father, worried? That's a joke. (*To* **Edward**.) Now, sire, you won't get past the gates of the palace in those rags.

**Edward**   I suppose not. And my sister Elizabeth would never let me forget it.

**Miles**   Good. I'm going out to pick you up a new suit of clothes. You wait here and rest.

**Edward**   Very well. But don't be too long. It's the royal banquet at Guildhall tonight and I'll be expected to attend.

**Miles** (*out*)   Poor little friendless rat. Who can blame a boy raised on violence for seeking escape in fantasy? He'll soon come right under my care.

*He bows and exits.*

**Edward** (*out*)   He seems like a decent fellow. He has manners and breeding, at least. And he fought that devil Canty like a true knight.

*He begins to fence with an invisible sword and an invisible enemy.*

Take that, John Canty, you filthy fopdoodle. And that, you stinking slopface . . .

**John Canty** *appears at the window. He stealthily climbs in and tiptoes towards* **Edward***, who is too engaged in his game to notice.*

**Edward** (*to his invisible foe*)    One day your head will be on a spike, you mangy maltworm, and then what will you do?

**Canty**    Why, son, I'll grin at you from ear to ear.

**Edward** *screams.* **Canty** *grabs him and carries him out.*

**Scene Thirteen**

*The* **Busker** *appears as the scene changes to the Thames side.*

**Busker**
    The Thames, the Thames, the noble Thames
    The heart of London city
    Behold her gleaming merchant ships
    Her palaces so pretty
    The Thames, the Thames, the royal Thames
    The pride of London town
    But if you fall into her arms
    She'll pull your body down.

*The Royal Barge appears carrying* **Tom** *and* **Elizabeth***. The* **Crowd** *cheers.*

**Tom**    Are all these people at the riverside really here to see me?

**Elizabeth**    Of course they are, Edward. Now remember the wave I showed you?

**Tom**    The royal flick?

**Elizabeth**    No, the Tudor twirl.

*She demonstrates.* **Tom** *copies her. The barge docks.*

**Crowd**
> He waved at me, did you see that
> He's the people's prince all right
> Funny-looking hands, the Tudors, eh
> It's all the tennis, probably.

*The* **Crowd** *cheers as* **Tom** *steps off the barge, followed by* **Elizabeth**. **Lord Hertford** *is waiting to meet them.*

**Tom** (*out*)   This could be my chance to escape. I could jump overboard and swim back to Offal Court.

**Hertford**   Step fast, my lord. I must speak with you most urgently.

**Tom** (*out*)   If I don't go now, I'll be bound for ever to King Henry's promise.

**Hertford**   Sire, your father is gone.

*A bugle note sounds, long and forlorn.*

**Messenger** (*voice-over*)   Grievous news! Henry, King of England, Ireland and Wales, royal sovereign, defender of the faith, is dead. Long live the king.

*Hush descends. Everyone kneels before* **Edward**.

**Elizabeth**   Our father is dead. Long live King Edward, ruler of all England.

**Tom**   But I can't be king! There's been a dreadful mistake.

**Hertford**   Your Majesty, you must address your people.

**Elizabeth**   Yes, Edward, show them you mean business.

*She pushes him forward. A microphone descends.* **Tom** *addresses the* **Crowd**.

**Tom**   H-h-hello . . .

**Elizabeth**   Command them, Edward. Your word is law.

**Tom**   It is?

**Hertford**   Indeed, Your Majesty. See how they kneel in your honour.

**Tom** (*into the mic*)   Good people, you must not kneel for me!

**Elizabeth**   Steady on, Edward.

**Tom**   I may be king but I'm still one of them. (*To the* **Crowd**.) Arise, I tell you, until I have proved myself worthy.

**Hertford**   The king has spoken. Arise for King Edward, the true ruler of all England.

*The* **Crowd**, *astonished, stands up.*

**All**   Long live King Edward, the true ruler of all England!

> The king, the king, the noble king
> The pride of London city
> Behold his noble countenance
> His manners oh so pretty
> The king, the king, the royal king
> A boy of truest mercy
> Although he's only nine years old
> We'll serve him faithfully.

## Act Two

*The troupe of actors reassembles and waits for the audience to settle. As they perform the opening song they put on their costumes and set the stage for Act Two.*

### Scene Fourteen

*A forest.* **John Canty** *and* **Hobbs**, *a thief, reel around the fire singing drunkenly.* **Edward** *stands nearby, his hands tied. As they sing he tries to edge away.*

*Song: 'The Fireside Song'.*

**Canty/Hobbs**
We're dells, we're budges, we're doxies
We're maunders and dudgeons and files
We beg for our bread and fight for our kicks
And we live by our wits and our wiles

We're ruffians of the highway
We've naught but our cunning and gall
Our only jewels are our knives and our sticks
But we're kings and princes all.

*They clink tankards.*

**Hobbs**   What brings you out to the countryside, John? It's a while since I've seen you in these parts.

**Canty**   I had to skip town for a while. (*Proudly.*) No common thief, I no more. I'm a murderer now.

**Hobbs**   Oh, yeah? Who d'you kill?

**Canty**   A rent collector.

**Hobbs**   Nice.

**Canty**   He had it coming. Charging me interest on the rent I owe! It's daylight robbery.

**Hobbs**   So what d'you do?

**Canty**   I shanked him and stole his purse. Like I said, daylight robbery.

*They cackle.* **Canty** *spots* **Edward** *creeping away and yanks him back.*

**Edward**   I'll see you're punished properly one day, John Canty.

**Canty**   Shut it! (*He cuffs* **Edward**.) Kicking and fighting me all the way from London. You should see me, Hobbs, I'm black and blue.

**Edward**   It's no more than you deserve, you brute.

**Hobbs**   Bit fresh, ain't he? Who is the lad, anyway? He's a fine-looking boy.

**Canty**   He's my son. Don't worry, he'll pay his way. I'll put him to work tomorrow.

**Hobbs**   Aye, with a face like that he'll tug at the heartstrings of many a lonely old man.

**Edward**   I am not your son.

**Canty**   Oh, yeah, I forgot. Tell Mr Hobbs who you are, boy.

**Edward**   I am Edward, Prince of Wales.

**Hobbs**   Well, why didn't you say, John? We can't have the poor noble lad trussed up like this.

*He undoes* **Edward***'s ropes, winking at* **Canty**. **Edward** *rubs his wrists.*

**Edward**   At last, a bit of common courtesy.

**Hobbs**   And that's not all, Yer Highness. A prince needs a royal sceptre. (*He thrusts a stick of wood in* **Edward***'s hand.*) And a royal throne. (*He plonks him on a barrel.*) And last but not least, a royal crown.

*He crowns* **Edward** *with a tin saucepan.*

**Edward**   When my father King Henry gets his hands on you, you'll wish you'd never mocked me so.

**Hobbs**   He won't though, will he? The old bugger's finally carked it.

**Canty**   Eh?

**Hobbs**   He died this afternoon. Good riddance to bad rubbish, I say. (*He spits.*)

**Edward**   Liar! The king is alive and well.

**Hobbs**   It's no lie. I heard the proclamation myself from the palace walls.

**Canty**   Then let's hope the greedy old git's gone straight to hell. (*He spits.*)

**Edward**   It cannot be! My poor papa . . .

**Hobbs**   What's he so upset about? Bit of a royalist, is he, your boy?

**Canty**   He's a nincompoop, that's what he is.

*He ties* **Edward** *up again.*

**Canty**   I'm your poor papa, and you'll do as I say, boy. You're my witness to murder. If I go down, you go down with me.

**Hobbs**   You know what they say. Families that slay together, stay together.

**Canty** *and* **Hobbs** *roll themselves in blankets.* **Edward** *looks up at the sky.*

**Edward**   If you are watching from heaven, Father, send help, I beg you. For if you are gone then truly I am lost.

*The* **Busker** *appears and sings quietly.*

**Busker**
    Poor King Edward, pauper's son
    Poor King Edward on the run
    No more silk and cloth of gold
    Just a bed that's hard and cold

Here's a blanket made of rain
Here's a lullaby of pain
Here's a sheet that's spun from fear
Here's a pillow damp with tears

Poor King Edward, all alone
Poor King Edward, far from home
No more hope of brave rescue
Just a heart that's broke in two.


## Scene Fifteen

*Guildhall, night. A table is set for a banquet.* **Tom** *enters ceremonially, followed by* **Elizabeth**, *the* **Chancellor** *and* **Hertford**.

**Chancellor**    Everything to your liking, Your Majesty?

**Tom**    It looks just like the pictures in my book about life at court!

**Hertford**    Very good, sire. Are you ready to meet your guests?

*Two foreign* **Ambassadors** *step forward.*

**Hertford**    May I present the French Ambassador and the Spanish Ambassador. His Majesty King Edward the Sixth.

*The* **Ambassadors** *bow to* **Tom**. *A* **Servant** *steps forward and offers them a tray of foil-wrapped sweetmeats.*

**Tom**    What are they?

**Hertford**    Sweetmeats, Your Majesty.

**Elizabeth**    Ambassadors' receptions are noted in society for their host's exquisite taste.

*The Ferrero Rocher advert theme plays as the* **Ambassadors** *eat their sweetmeats.*

**French Ambassador**    *Délicieuses.*

**Spanish Ambassador**    *Excelente.*

**French Ambassador**    Monsieur, with these riches you are really spoiling us.

*There's a sudden commotion outside – a mob cheering.* **Tom** *goes to the window.*

**Tom**    What's that noise?

**Chancellor**    A procession to the gallows, sire. Some lowly villain going to meet his fate.

**Tom**    Death by hanging! A terrible thing.

**Hertford**    Fear is the best deterrent for crime, my lord, as well your father knew.

**Tom**    But, listen, the man calls out his innocence.

**Beggar 2** (*off*)    I'm innocent!

**Tom**    Bring him to me.

*The company gasps, scandalised. The* **Chancellor** *takes* **Tom** *aside.*

**Chancellor**    Sire . . . is this wise? We must show the Ambassadors the firm hand of the English law, not that you dally with criminals.

**Tom**    We must be sure he *is* a criminal before we send him to his death.

**Hertford**    Very well, Your Majesty.

*He leaves.* **Tom** *waves the* **Ambassadors** *towards a pile of fruit.*

**Tom**    Ambassadors, try that while we're waiting, it's called a pine apple.

**Elizabeth** *and the* **Chancellor** *hiss at him.*

**Chancellor**    Not the pine apple, Your Majesty!

**Elizabeth**    You're forgetting everything I've taught you, Edward!

**Tom** (*to the* **Ambassadors**)    Oh, yes. Forgive me. Not the pine apple. It's only for show. We've got to give it back at the end of the week.

*The* **Ambassadors** *turn away and confer.*

**French Ambassador**    It seems the rumours of King Edward's madness are true.

**Spanish Ambassador**    *Si*. He is not, as they say, the full shilling.

**Hertford** *enters with* **Beggar 2**, *who prostrates himself before* **Tom**.

**Tom**    Well? Of what does he stand accused?

**Hertford**    Murder, Your Majesty. He killed a rent collector.

**All**    Ooooh!

**Tom**    And his punishment?

**Hertford**    To be boiled alive in oil, Your Majesty.

**All**    Errrrrgh!

**Tom**    Boiled alive? Like a pudding? What a dreadful way to go.

**Beggar 2**    Oh spare me, your royal gloriousness. It wasn't me who killed the rent collector, I swear.

**All**    Eh?

**Beggar 2**    It was John Canty what done it, everyone knows that. He was boasting about it down the Lamb and Flag.

**Tom**    John Canty! My – (*He stops himself.*) My goodness. Let the prisoner go free. It is the king's will.

**Hertford**    My lord? How can you be sure he's telling the truth?

**Tom**    An educated guess. Good man, no oil shall boil for you. Nor any man while I am king. Go back to your job with my blessing.

**Beggar 2**    God bless you, King Edward, sir! I'd give my right arm for a job.

**All**    You haven't got a right arm.

**Beggar 2**    Whatever.

**Tom** *gives the beggar the pineapple.*

**Tom**    Take this, then. You can sell it for a goodly sum.

**Beggar 2** (*unimpressed*)    Oh, thank you, your royal blessedness.

**Chancellor**    But sire – we can't afford it! That pine apple's worth its weight in gold.

**Tom**    We'll sell something to pay the owner. (*He takes off his cloak.*) I'd rather go without cloth of gold than see a poor man starve.

*Everyone applauds. The* **Ambassadors** *confer.*

**Spanish Ambassador**    The new king is no madman. In fact his wits seem very sound.

**French Ambassador**    And no weakling, either, but a man of strength and honour.

*They exit.*

**Hertford**    Your deed has impressed the Ambassadors more than any pine apple, Your Majesty. Such mercy has sown valuable seeds.

**Tom**    A king is more than fine clothes and courtly manners, Lord Hertford. Now let the feast begin!

*The* **Busker** *appears and sings.*

**Busker**
What's the point of a banquet, if the food just goes to waste?
What's the point of a pineapple, if you'll never have a taste?
What's the point of riches, if your spirit's poor?
What's the point of power, if you don't know what it's for?

## Scene Sixteen

*Morning.* **Canty** *and* **Edward** *are setting up their begging pitch in a country lane.*

**Canty**    We'll work the crumpled cripple con this morning while Hobbs is at market picking pockets. Remember how to do it?

**Edward**    If you're asking me to beg, the answer's never. I would not stoop so low!

**Canty**    You never used to be this difficult. I knew letting you read all them books was a mistake.

**Edward**    That's the least of your mistakes. I'd be more worried about the liberties you've taken with the King of England.

**Canty** *grabs* **Edward** *by the scruff of the neck.*

**Canty**    For the last time will you stop this poxy make-believe!

*A* **Woman** *enters on her way to market, carrying a basket.* **Canty** *drops to the floor and pretends he has no legs.*

**Canty**    Spare any change? Help a man in trouble?

**Woman**    What ails you, poor fellow? Shall I fetch a surgeon?

**Canty**    Nay, there's no money for surgeons. I must suffer my affliction while my only son starves.

**Woman**    Poor lad. Here, eat this. (*She takes a bun from her basket and tosses it to* **Edward**.) How long's your father been legless?

**Edward** *eats the bun.*

**Edward**    He's always legless, madam, and he's not my father. He's a liar and a thief.

**Woman**    What?

**Canty**    Pay no attention, lady, my son's witless. He likes to pretend he's a prince.

**Edward**    A king, actually! (*To the* **Woman**.) Do I look like a beggar to you?

**Woman**    Yes.

**Edward**    Well, you shall have to take my word that I'm not. Do you have another bun?

**Woman**    You're as bad as each other. Taking advantage of my kind heart and my simple nature.

**Canty**    We're swindlers, love, that's the whole point.

**Woman**    Then you should be ashamed of yourselves.

*She kicks* **Canty**, *who groans.*

**Edward**    Well said.

**Canty** *leaps up, grabbing* **Edward**.

**Canty**    I've had it with you!

*He throws a sack over the* **Woman**'s *head and grabs her basket, spinning her around to confuse her. While she's shrieking and stumbling about,* **Canty** *takes a roast piglet with an apple in its mouth from the basket.*

**Canty**    A dressed pig? That'll fetch a decent sum.

**Woman**    Don't take the piglet! It's to sell at market so I can feed my children.

**Edward**    Give it back to her, you villain.

*He grabs the piglet from* **Canty** *as the* **Woman** *throws off her sack.*

**Woman** (*to* **Edward**)    Thief! Give me back my pig.

**Edward**    I don't want it! Here, take it.

*He throws the piglet back to the* **Woman** *but* **Canty** *steps in and catches it.*

**Canty**    He's lying. The boy's a thieving knave just like his father.

*He removes the apple and takes a bite before throwing the piglet back to* **Edward**.

**Canty**    Catch this.

**Edward**    I will not!

**Woman**    Don't drop it, I beg you – it'll get spoiled. Help!

**Edward** *has no choice but to catch the pig. A* **Constable** *appears, followed by a crowd.*

**Canty**    It's the law! (*To* **Edward**.) Toodle pip! Better you rot in jail than hinder me any longer.

*He runs away full pelt. The* **Woman** *snatches her piglet from* **Edward**.

**Woman**    You box of rubbish, you! Stealing from a poor woman.

**Edward**    I was not I. It was him.

**Constable**    Who?

**Crowd**    Yeah, who?

**Edward** *looks around but* **Canty** *is long gone. The* **Crowd** *closes in on* **Edward**.

**Crowd**
 Take the boy to the magistrate
 Give him the birch or the stocks
 Hand him over to us instead
 We'll give his ears a box
 Lock him up in a prison cell
 Poke him with a stick
 And if he won't apologise
 We'll clobber him with bricks.

*They push and pull at him like feral animals. They chant, half hypnotised.*

 Punish him!
 Beat him!
 Pelt him!

Whip him!
Flog him!
Lash him!
Hurt him!
Slap him!

**Miles** *appears.*

**Miles**    Let the boy go!

*The* **Crowd** *stops to look at* **Miles**. **Edward** *gasps.*

**Edward**    M –

**Miles** *claps a hand over* **Edward**'s *mouth.*

**Constable**    Know this boy do you, sir?

**Miles**    No, never set eyes on him. But I can tell he's from decent stock.

**Woman**    Decent stock? He tried to steal my piglet.

**Edward** *protests through* **Miles**'s *fingers.* **Miles** *clamps down harder.*

**Miles**    Is it not returned to its rightful owner? I'll take the boy with me and be on my way.

**Constable**    Not so fast. The lad's a proven criminal. He'll come with me to the courthouse.

**Crowd**
Punish him!
Beat him!
Pelt him!
Whip him!
Flog him!
Lash him!
Hurt him!
Slap him –

**Miles**    Enough! That is not justice, it is revenge.

*The* **Crowd** *mutters, aggrieved.*

**Miles**   Let the law decide the punishment. I'll come with you to the magistrate to make sure he's treated fairly.

*He sets off with* **Edward**, *followed by the* **Crowd**.

**Edward**   How the devil did you find me, Miles?

**Miles**   It wasn't difficult. I just followed John Canty's trail of villainous deeds from tavern to village to forest.

**Edward**   Thank God for your wits. And Miles, one other thing –

**Miles**   What, sire?

**Edward**   Never let it get out that the King of England was brought down by a dressed pig. I'd be the laughing stock of the country.


**Scene Seventeen**

*Palace. The* **Chancellor** *and* **Hertford** *sit* **Tom** *at a desk, which is piled with papers. They hand* **Tom** *documents, which he signs and passes on.*

*Song: 'The Royal Admin Song'.*

**Chancellor**
  Letters, laws and legalities
  Arrangements, affairs and appeals
  Petitions and proclamations
  Deliveries, debts and deals

**Hertford**
  Missives, minutes and messages
  Summonses, statutes and sales
  Public papers, patents and polls
  For England and for Wales

**Chancellor** *and* **Hertford**
  Papers high as the sky above
  Blocking out the sun

All must feel the quill
Royal Admin must be done.

**Tom** *nods off, worn out.* **Hertford** *gives* **Tom** *a nudge.*

**Hertford**    Sire, there are still many matters that require your attention.

**Tom**    More?

**Chancellor**    Yes, sire. And with the Royal Seal lost, you must sign every one in person.

**Tom** (*out*)    Here we go again with the Royal Seal. (*To the* **Chancellor**.) Did King Henry not tell of its whereabouts in his will?

**Chancellor**    No, sire.

**Tom**    And nobody at court has seen it since his death?

**Hertford**    Indeed not, sire. Its disappearance is a mystery. Let us hope we find it anon.

**Tom**    Anon?

**Hertford**    Anon . . . 'soon', sire. (*To the* **Chancellor**.) His memory has not yet recovered.

**Chancellor**    Perhaps that's just as well. Sign here please, Your Majesty.

**Tom** *is about to – then stops, and studies the paper.*

**Tom**    What is this one for?

**Chancellor**    Court expenses, Your Majesty.

**Tom**    How much are they?

*The* **Chancellor** *nods discreetly at* **Hertford**.

**Chancellor**    Twenty-eight thousand, Your Majesty.

**Hertford** *coughs strategically over the 'thousand'.*

**Tom**    How much?

**Chancellor**    Twenty-eight thousand.

**Hertford** *coughs as before.*

**Tom**    Twenty-eight pounds?

**Chancellor**    Yes, twenty-eight thousand.

**Hertford** *coughs again.*

**Tom**    Are you quite all right, Lord Hertford?

**Chancellor**    Just sign here, Your Majesty, and it will be dealt with.

**Tom** *stares at the paper.*

**Tom**    Twenty-eight *thousand* pounds! What the hell did you spend it on?

**Hertford**    Food and drink. Clothes and furnishings. The court must keep up appearances, sire.

**Tom**    Who for?

**Chancellor**    The ordinary people of England, sire, who rejoice to know their ruler is kept in kingly style.

**Tom**    But if we cut down on court expenses, we could pay off King Henry's debts and have plenty left for a banquet or two.

**Chancellor** *(tartly)*    Not to mention the odd pine apple.

**Tom**    What is a pine apple to a tax on the poor that feeds this court while they starve in the street? Greed breeds greed, gentlemen, I have seen it first hand. If the common people must go without, then so should we.

**Hertford**    Very well, Your Majesty.

**Chancellor**    If I could just have the papers you've already signed.

*He reaches for the signed papers, but* **Tom** *takes them away.*

**Tom**    I think I'll take a closer look at these before they are sent out. Now call for the Court Accountant. I should like to see his ledgers.

**Hertford** *and the* **Chancellor** *bow and withdraw.*

**Chancellor**    What do we do, Lord Hertford? This is a disaster!

**Hertford**    It's clear the king's mind is still weak. But perhaps his ideas are not.

**Chancellor**    Are you mad? At this rate the court will be ruined.

**Hertford**    And yet the lives of the poor might be rebuilt.

**Chancellor**    Whatever.


**Scene Eighteen**

*The courthouse.* **Edward** *is in the dock with the* **Constable***, the* **Woman** *is in the witness box.* **Miles** *watches. The* **Judge** *bangs his gavel.*

**Judge**    Silence in court! What is your name, boy?

**Edward**    Edward, your honour.

**Judge**    Edward what, boy?

**Edward**    Edward King of –

**Miles** *coughs.* **Edward** *stops.*

**Judge**    Edward Kingov. An unusual name. Well, Master Kingov, you stand accused of stealing a dressed pig. What have you to say?

**Edward**    I say the good woman is mistaken.

**Judge**    Mistaken, eh? And what does the victim answer to that?

**Woman**    We caught him red-handed, your honour. He was cradling my piglet like a newborn babe.

**Judge**    And how much is the piglet worth?

**Woman**   It cost me three shillings and eightpence, sir.

*Everyone gasps.*

**Edward**   What is the matter?

**Judge**   The law states that when one steals an object above the value of three shillings –

**Miles**   He shall hang for it!

**Edward**   Hang for it?

**Judge**   Hang for it.

**Edward**   That can't be right! What sort of a law would send someone to death for such a paltry sum?

**Judge**   King Henry's law, my boy, that's what.

**Woman**   I was mistaken, your honour! The pig cost me eightpence and not a penny more.

*Everyone sighs with relief.* **Miles** *throws his arms around the* **Woman** *and kisses her.*

**Miles**   Let me kiss you for your mercy, good woman. You're a kind and loving spirit.

**Judge**   So be it. The value of the pig is recorded as eightpence, and all that remains is to find a reasonable punishment. Let the boy take six weeks in prison.

**Miles**   Very good, your honour. I'm sure a spell in the country jail will set the boy on a different path.

**Edward**   Six weeks in prison! But I didn't do anything wrong.

**Miles**   Hush, lad. Would I betray you now? Thank you, your honour, we are much obliged.

**Judge**   Let me write up the record. Off you go, good wife, and repossess your porcine prize.

**Woman**   You what, sir?

**Judge**    Your pig, my dear, your pig. Court dismissed!

*The* **Woman** *curtseys and takes the pig. The* **Constable** *opens the door for her and follows her outside.* **Miles** *and* **Edward** *confer.*

**Edward**    What shall we do? I'll die in prison, surely!

**Miles**    Give me a minute to think, lad. I'll take some air to clear my head.

**Miles** *exits. Outside, he listens unseen as the* **Constable** *approaches the* **Woman**.

**Constable**    It's a fine-looking pig all right. Will you sell it to me? I'll give you eightpence for it.

**Woman**    Eightpence? I paid three shillings and eightpence for it, didn't you just hear me say so?

**Constable**    I heard you say 'eightpence', madam, and that was under oath. Does that mean *you lied in court*? If I tell the judge, you'll hang for it.

**Woman**    You sneaky wretch! Is that what I get for showing human charity? Take the pig. Anything to save the boy's life.

*She hands over the pig and exits, crying. The* **Constable** *hides it near the door, and goes back into the courthouse rubbing his hands.*

**Miles** (*out*)    The cheeky scoundrel! Now I have means for our escape.

*He puts the pig under his coat, then goes inside.*

**Judge**    The record is written and the sentence passed. Constable, take the boy to the county jail.

**Miles**    I'll walk along with the boy, sir, if I may.

**Judge**    As you like. Well, Master Kingov, off you go, then, and don't let me see you again.

**Edward** *steps down and the* **Constable** *leads him out of the courthouse.* **Miles** *follows. As they walk,* **Miles** *sings a little song.*

**Miles**

> I had a little piggy
> Nothing did she wear
> But a strip of bacon
> Across her back so fair

*The* **Constable** *gives him a funny look.*

> She held a little apple
> Within her cheeks so fat
> And if her worth is eightpence
> I'll up and eat my hat.

*The* **Constable** *stops walking.*

**Miles**    Why have we stopped? Don't you have a pig to collect once you've delivered the lad to jail?

**Constable** (*guiltily*)    A pig? What pig?

**Miles** *pulls the pig out of his jacket.*

**Miles**    This one.

**Constable** (*out*)    Oh heck.

**Miles**    I heard what you did back there in court. You blackmailing blackguard.

*He draws his sword.*

**Constable**    I'm not a bad man, sir. I thought I'd sell it in the market. My wife is sick, I need money for her medicines.

**Miles**    I doubt the judge will care a whit. And seeing as the pig was heard to be worth three shillings and eightpence, he'll sentence you to hang instead.

**Constable**    Me, hang?

**Miles**    It's what the law decrees for blackmail. (*Solemnly.*) *Ego clamo, vos clamatis, omnes clamamus pro glace lactis.*

**Edward** (*out*)    I scream, you scream, we all scream for ice cream?

**Miles** *shushes* **Edward**.

**Constable**    Won't you spare me, sir? I can't leave my poor wife a widow.

**Miles**    Very well. But in exchange you must let the boy escape. Now close your eyes and count to a hundred. By the time you've finished we'll be gone.

**Constable**    But I can't count past ten, sir. I never had much schooling.

**Miles**    Then count to ten ten times over – it amounts to the same thing.

**Constable**    Ooh, that's good advice. I'll remember that one.

*He covers his eyes and begins to count.* **Miles** *unties* **Edward**'s *hands.*

**Edward**    You lied to him, Miles! That's not the act of a gentleman.

**Miles**    You'll learn, lad. Sometimes lies are necessary to preserve justice. Now come on. *Veni, vidi, vamos.*

**Scene Nineteen**

*Palace.* **Edward**'s *chambers.* **Tom** *signs his last paper.*

**Tom**    Finished! All revised, rewritten, and re-signed! (*Out.*) I don't mind being king, but it does take up an awful lot of time. And it's a lonely job, besides.

*He stands, yawns, scratches. He sees the suit of armour, bows to it.*

Brave knight, will you joust with me a while? (*As the knight.*) It will be my honour, Your Majesty. (*As* **Tom**.) Then draw arms and approach.

*He fights with the suit of armour.*

You won't fight? Then surrender your arms.

*The Royal Seal falls out of the suit of armour. He picks it up.*

Ah. It's the nutcracker. This will come in handy. I still don't see the point of a fork or a knife. And a spoon was never any use in Offal Court where there's no food to eat it with. (*Out.*) I can't pretend that I don't remember my other life. But Offal Court seems a million miles away now. And if my new laws help the poor, perhaps my mother and sister – even my father – might have a better life. (*He pockets the Seal.*) 1 may be a lonely king, but at least I'm a busy one. It's up to me now to set this kingdom to rights.

## Scene Twenty

**Miles** *and* **Edward** *trudge on through the countryside.*

*Song: 'The Travelling Song'.*

### Miles

Only another half mile now, sonny
Soon we'll be home to Hendon Hall
No finer house in the whole of the land
The best you ever saw

### Edward

But I miss my sister Lizzie
Even though she drove me mad
And I miss my poor dead father, Miles
The best I ever had.

### Miles

Hendon Hall has sixty chambers
Sixty servants to wait on you
They'll rub you down and they'll dress you up
And make you good as new

### Edward

Good Miles Hendon, true and kind
A noble man I have no doubt

But I must return to the palace soon
And kick the false king out.

**Miles**    There are the gates, lad, look! And behind them is
Lady Edith. How I've missed her.

**Edward**    Is Edith your wife?

**Miles**    Not yet. But we'll be married soon enough. And
you'll meet my dear father, Sir Richard. And my brother
Hugh. He's high-spirited at times, but he means well.

**Edward** *sighs.*

**Miles**    What is troubling you, lad?

**Edward**    Why have *I* not been missed, Miles? Doesn't
anyone care that I've disappeared?

**Miles**    Never mind that now, sire. Here's the watchman.
Welcome to Hendon Hall!

*The house gates appear. A blind* **Watchman** *stands outside.* **Miles**
*gives him a penny.*

**Miles**    Good morrow, friend. It's been seven long years since
we last met.

**Watchman**    I've never set eyes on you in my life, sir. I'm
blind as a dormouse since the master whipped me for falling
asleep on my watch.

**Miles** (*to* **Edward**)    The poor man's mind wanders. My
father would never have whipped a man blind. (*To the*
**Watchman**.) Well then, I'm Miles Hendon, of Hendon Hall,
returned to home and hearth.

**Watchman**    Oh, lawks. (*Out.*) This means trouble, and no
mistake.

*He exits.*

**Miles**    Strange fellow. Come lad, let's go in.

*They enter the house. In the hallway* **Hugh** *sits at a desk, writing.*

**Miles**   Hugh, is that you? It is I, Miles, returned at last. And this is my ward.

**Hugh** *stares at* **Miles**.

**Hugh**   Your wits must be touched, poor stranger. I have no brother Miles.

**Miles** (*to* **Edward**)   Didn't I tell you the man has spirits? (*To* **Hugh**.) Enough of your jokes, Hugh, come and embrace your brother.

**Hugh**   You heartless knave. Miles Hendon was killed in battle. We received a letter seven years ago.

**Miles**   Killed? What am I then, a ghost? Now call Father, I long to see him.

**Hugh**   One may not call the dead.

**Miles**   Dead?

**Hugh**   Our father – my father – died last winter. A plague took him, and most of the servants.

**Miles**   This is heavy news. I beg you, do not say the Lady Edith –

**Hugh**   Lady Edith is alive and well.

**Miles**   Thank God. Where is she? She will not deny me, even if you will.

**Hugh**   We'll see about that.

*He exits.*

**Miles**   This is not the homecoming I had planned upon.

**Edward**   No, indeed. Where are the sixty servants and the warm welcome?

**Miles**   I don't know, lad. It troubles me too.

**Edward**   In faith, how am I to know you are who you say you are?

**Miles**    Don't tell me you doubt me too?

**Edward** *looks into* **Miles**' *eyes.*

**Edward**    No. I do not doubt you, Miles.

**Miles** *clasps* **Edward**'s *hands.*

**Miles**    Thank you my little king. Edith will confirm it, wait and see.

**Hugh** *enters with* **Edith** *and the* **Watchman**. **Miles** *runs to* **Edith**.

**Miles**    Edith, my darling –

**Hugh** *holds him off.*

**Hugh**    Look upon this man, Edith. Do you know him?

**Edith** *looks at* **Miles** *quickly, then away.*

**Edith**    I do not.

**Miles**    Edith?

*She stifles a sob and runs from the room.*

**Hugh**    You see, sir. You are a stranger to my wife.

**Miles**    Your *wife*?

*He leaps to his feet and gets* **Hugh** *against the wall, throttling him.*

**Miles**    You fox-hearted slave! There is some treachery at work here, yet I know not what.

**Hugh**    Help!

*A crowd of* **Peasants** *enters and restrains* **Miles** *and* **Edward**.

**Hugh**    How dare you insult my good name? (*He takes out a cosh and whacks* **Miles** *on the head.*) Take this vagabond to the village square.

*The* **Peasants** *carry* **Miles** *off.*

**Edward**    You can't do that – you're no magistrate.

**Hugh**    I can do what I like, boy. I have the running of this house and the village, too. Didn't King Henry himself grant me my powers?

**Edward**    My father would never have done that. He'd have seen you were a bad lot!

**Hugh**    Another fantasist in our midst. Perhaps you'll learn some sense when you see your master punished.

**Peasants**
>  Why not lash the boy himself
>  Give him a taste of leather
>  Bring him down off his high horse
>  Show him he ain't so clever
>
>  Take him to the village square
>  It ain't a moment too soon
>  When he sees what awaits him there
>  He's sure to change his tune.


**Scene Twenty-One**

*Village square. The crowd holds* **Miles** *and* **Edward** *apart.* **Hugh** *stands by with* **Lady Edith**.

**Edward**    Leave him alone. He is a servant of the king!

**Miles**    Ignore him, everyone, he's mad as a squirrel!

**Edward**    But Miles –

**Miles**    You'll destroy us, lad. Keep your trap shut.

**Edward**    I won't!

*He launches himself at the crowd. They catch him and pinion his arms.*

**Edith**    Let the child go, Hugh. Can't you see how young and frail he is?

**Hugh**    Frail? He's savage as a mongrel. Let's whip the boy, and see if we can't tame him.

**Crowd**    Yeah!

**Miles**    I beg you no, Hugh. I will take the lashes for him.

**Hugh**    Now that's a good idea. Give the impostor an honest dozen.

**Edward**    If you lay one finger on Miles I'll have the lot of you boiled in oil!

**Hugh**    And for every word you speak from now on, boy, he'll take six strokes more.

*The* **Watchman** *whips* **Miles** *before the gleeful crowd.*

**Crowd**
One, two, three, four
See the blood begin to pour
Five, six, seven, eight
Watch the blighter start to shake
Nine, ten and eleven
He's in hell but we're in heaven
Twelve strokes put to bed
Hold him up, man, is he dead?
(*Pause.*) Shame!

*The* **Watchman** *releases* **Miles**. **Edward** *rushes to him, crying, and covers his back.*

**Edward**    Oh brave and noble Miles. Never did I imagine a friend would take such blows for me.

**Miles**    Don't worry lad, I'll live.

**Edward**    You will never take the like again, but all men shall know of your nobility.

*He picks up a stick and touches* **Miles** *on the shoulder.*

**Edward**    Edward King of England dubs thee Earl. Arise Lord Hendon, most heroic of men.

*He helps* **Miles** *up.*

**Miles**    I'll say something for you, Your Majesty – you never give up.

**Hugh**    If you've finished your little love-fest, I think it's time you were on your way.

**Miles**    You may have fooled these people, Hugh, but you don't fool me. While I languished in my foreign prison, you plotted to steal all that was rightfully mine.

**Hugh** (*to the* **Crowd**)    See how the knave maintains he is my brother? (*To* **Miles**.) This forgery will get you nowhere.

**Miles**    Forgery! Of course! You wrote the letter about my death yourself. All so you could get your hands on my bride. Take that!

*He lands a punch on* **Hugh**. **Hugh** *reels. The* **Crowd** *gasps.*

**Hugh**    Throw him in jail.

*The* **Crowd** *cheers. The* **Watchman** *grabs* **Miles**.

**Miles** (*to* **Edward**)    I'm sorry I let you down, lad. You should have saved yourself when you had the chance.

**Edward**    No king would abandon a friend in his hour of need. If you must die in prison, I'll die with you.

*The* **Watchman** *drags* **Miles** *off.* **Edward** *follows.* **Edith** *stands weeping.*

**Crowd**
Don't upset yourself, Lady Edith.
They're just a couple of pesky criminals.
No use crying over spilt blood.

**Edith**    Whoever they are, they are human beings. When will we learn to show some mercy to our fellow man?

*She exits. The* **Crowd** *stands scratching their heads, perplexed.*

**Crowd**
I suppose it's all right, mercy
I suppose it does no harm

I suppose it don't cost nothing
To turn on a little charm
I've heard it's the rage in London
So should we try it too?
All right then, after you, love
Oh no, dear, after you.


## Scene Twenty-Two

*The palace. The royal* **Tailor** *is fitting* **Tom** *for his Coronation gown.*

**Tailor**    Are we sure we don't want the ermine trim, Your Majesty? Your father had the same on his Coronation gown, and a lovelier sight I never saw.

**Tom**    I'll make do without. We must watch the royal pennies.

**Tailor**    The public does love a good show of luxury, sire.

**Tom**    The public can't even afford to pay their rent, thanks to King Henry's greed. Why should they love me in ermine they'll never get to touch?

**Elizabeth** *bursts in.*

**Elizabeth**    Edward, a word! Lord Chancellor has just told me I am not to have a new gown for the Coronation.

**Tailor**    He's economising, Lady Elizabeth.

**Elizabeth**    Would you rather I dressed in rags like a common beggar?

**Tom**    This is no time to boast about our royal wealth, dear sister. We must show the people we understand the sacrifices they have made.

**Elizabeth**    What next, Edward? Show all the criminals in this country you understand why they broke the law?

**Tom**   That's a good idea. (*He scribbles a note and gives it to* **Elizabeth**.) Take this to the Chancellor and tell him it must go to every magistrate in every county.

**Elizabeth**   What is it?

**Tom**   A royal decree. Half the tenants of every prison will be released tomorrow in honour of my Coronation.

**Elizabeth**   Edward, this mercy drive has got to stop! You've already pardoned three hundred murderers, five hundred thieves and seven hundred hooligans. And that's just since Tuesday.

**Tom**   I looked at the court records. Half of them were wrongly imprisoned. The other half were women and children whose only crime was poverty and hunger.

**Elizabeth**   What is this passion you have for beggars, all of a sudden?

**Tom**   It is just a respect for the working man.

**Elizabeth**   But you're not a working man! You're a king!

**Tom**   Even a king must try to understand how the common people live. Good day, Elizabeth. I must attend to the Coronation budget.

*He bows and leaves.*

**Tailor**   Don't you worry, my lady. I'll stitch a new trim on your old gown, and no one shall know the difference. When times are hard we must all make do and mend.

**Elizabeth**   But I'm a princess, not a pauperess. Edward has taken things too far.

**Tailor**   You know what they say, ma'am. Families that save together wave together.

**Elizabeth**   Fiddlesticks. If I ever become queen, I shall make sure the royal court flourishes and my gowns will be the envy of all Europe. Hit it, minstrels.

*Song: 'If I Could Be Queen'.*

If I could be queen I'd make Britain great
An excellent nation of noble estate
So why don't you give me a royal audition
Cos there ain't nothing wrong with a little red ambition

When I am queen everything will be beautiful
Every Englishman dutiful and very keen
When I am queen I can do without pearls or lace
I'll be more than just a pretty face when I am queen

Not the sister of a king but a royal sovereign
No longer little Liz or gentle Bet
Queen Elizabeth's no girl, but the empress of the world
So pay your respects or I'll have to snip your curls

When I am queen everything will be excellent
Every Englishman reverent and very clean
When I am queen I can do without pearls or lace
I'll be more than just a pretty face when I am queen

All the people would my praises sing
I'd commission songs and plays and take a bard under
    my wing
For all the world's a stage and each must play his part
But if you mess up your lines you're on the execution cart

When I am queen everything will be glorious
Every Englishman victorious and full of beans
When I am queen I can do without pearls or lace
I'll be more than just a pretty face when I am queen.

**Tailor** (*out*)    Thank God that'll never happen.


## Scene Twenty-Three

*Prison.* **Miles** *and* **Edward** *share a cell with four* **Prisoners** *in chains.* **Miles** *paces.*

**Miles**    Edith, Edith, Edith . . . She could barely meet my eye. Surely that's a sign that she *did* know me?

**Prisoner 1**    Who'd trust a woman?

**Prisoner 2**    Here we go.

**Miles**    Hugh must have commanded her to lie on pain of death. That villain's stolen my future wife!

**Edward**    Who cares about your future wife? My whole life's been stolen!

**Miles**    Not now, lad. I'm in no mood for your fun and games.

**Edward**    Do I look as though I'm having fun?

**Miles**    Do I?

**Edward**    I asked you first!

**Miles**    Fantasist.

**Edward**    Impostor.

**Miles** and **Edward** *turn their backs to each other and walk off in opposite directions.*

**Prisoners**    Oooh!

**Miles** (*out*)    Poor brainsoft little lad. It's not his fault he lives in a dream.

**Edward** (*out*)    Poor heartsore earl. It's not his fault he's lost his betrothed.

**Edward/Miles**    Pax!

*They embrace.*

**Prisoners**    Ahhh.

**Miles**    I'll find a way out, sire. We don't deserve to fester in this filthy pit.

**Prisoner 4**    What about us?

**Edward**    That's different. You're criminals.

**Prisoner 1**    No we ain't. I was a farmer until King Henry stole my land to pay off his debts and made me homeless.

**Prisoner 2**    And I was a simple country widow until they accused me of witchcraft for growing herbs.

**Prisoner 3**    And I was an orphan girl forced to steal my bread.

**Prisoner 4**    And I lost my left arm in the plague.

**All**    Right arm.

**Edward**    So you'd rather thieve and cheat than make an honest living under the king's law?

**Prisoner 3**    There's nothing honest about the king's law. It protects the rich and punishes the poor.

**Prisoner 2**    Things might change when Edward's crowned. They say he's a boy with big ideas.

**Edward**    That little beggar boy, pretending to be *king*, now!

**Miles**    Hush, sire. We'll set things right once we escape.

**Prisoner 3**    Dream on, mister.

*The door creaks open. The* **Jailer** *shows in a figure in a hooded cloak.*

**Jailer**    Visitor for Hendon. Five minutes and no touching.

**Miles**    Who is it?

**Edith**    It is I, Lady Edith.

*Cue film music. The* **Prisoners** *take out hankies, popcorn, etc. They form an audience around* **Miles** *and* **Edith**.

**Prisoner 4**    Lady Edith, from Hendon Hall.

**Prisoner 3**    As fair as a summer meadow.

**Prisoner 1**    She's a real lady, all right.

**Prisoner 2**    A leading lady.

**Edith**    I have come to warn you, sir. You must stop your claim to be Miles Hendon.

**Miles**    Good heavens, Edith – I *am* Miles Hendon.

**Edith**    Please, good stranger. Sir Hugh will have you hanged for treason.

**Miles**    I only know one thing, Edith. That you loved me in the old days, as I did you. Look me in the eye and tell me I am not Miles.

**Edith**    You are not – (*She breaks off, unable to finish.*)

**Miles**    I knew it!

**Edith**    Oh, Miles, forgive me. When the news came that you were dead, I went mad with grief. Only after I was married I found drafts of the letter in Hugh's own hand and I knew he had arranged it all.

**Prisoners**    Shame.

**Miles**    I'll kill that scoundrel just as soon as we get out of here.

**Edith**    But we leave tonight for London. After the Coronation Hugh seeks an audience with the new king to ask for more land and power.

**Edward**    The Coronation?

**Edith**    King Edward will be crowned tomorrow at Westminster.

**Edward**    He's being crowned? *Tomorrow?* Miles, we must get back to London at once!

**Miles**    Aye, lad. If it's true that the new king favours the unfortunate, perhaps he will help restore my fortunes.

**Edward**    So what's our plan?

**Prisoner 1**    You need more than a plan, son – you need a miracle.

*The **Jailer** enters, holding up a parchment.*

**Jailer** (*grumpy*)    By Royal Decree of King Edward the Sixth, half the convicts in every English prison shall be released on this day.

**Prisoner 1**    God bless King Edward.

**Prisoner 2**    His mercy is no lie.

*They do a little dance of joy. Everyone hugs.*

**Miles**    London. here we come.

**Miles** *and* **Edward** *go to leave. The other* **Prisoners** *follow but the* **Jailer** *stops them.*

**Jailer**    Half the prisoners, the decree says, not all. Two of you can go, the other four must stay.

*He exits.*

**Prisoner 4**    That's not fair.

**Prisoner 3**    Yeah, that's a bad fraction.

**Miles**    Friends, I know we ask a lot. But if you let us go now, I promise I'll return anon to set you free.

**Prisoner 1**    I suppose we should give the young lad a chance.

**Prisoner 2**    And let the gentleman help Lady Edith.

**Edward**    I thank you, noble servants.

**Edith**    You can take my horse to speed your journey, and here's my cloak for disguise. Good luck, my love.

**Miles** *and* **Edith** *kiss.*

**All**    Ahhh.

**Edward**    Not now! We've no time to lose.

**Edward**, **Miles** *and* **Edith** *exit.* **Prisoner 2** *mops her eyes.*

**Prisoner 2**    I love a happy ending.

*Song: 'Lady Edith's Theme'.*

**Prisoners**
 Edith, Edith, a face like a flower in bloom
 Edith, Edith, you came not a moment too soon
 Edith, Edith, all that's left to do
 Edith, Edith, is escape your husband Hugh.

**Prisoner 1**    Edith, Edith, what I'd give for a lovely wife

**Prisoner 4 / 3**    Edith, Edith? (*Pointing to* **Prisoner 2**.) Why don't you use your eyes?

**Prisoner 2** *curtseys to* **Prisoner 1** *coquettishly.*

**Prisoner 2**
I'm no Edith, and a noble gent you're not
And yet we're chained together –

**Prisoner 1**
We may as well tie the knot!

**Prisoner 1** *gets down on one knee before* **Prisoner 2**. *She accepts him. They kiss.* **Prisoners 3** *and* **4** *sprinkle them with popcorn confetti.*

**Scene Twenty-Four**

*The Tower of London. A* **Crowd** *is gathered outside the gate. A* **Guard** *stands sentry.*

**Gentleman**    I say, any beheadings in the Tower today? I have my in-laws up for the Coronation, they want to see the sights.

**Guard**    Nah, no beheadings.

**Gentleman**    Any hangings?

**Guard**    Nah, no hangings.

**Gentleman**    Any floggings?

**Guard**    Ain't you heard? King Edward proclaimed the law of blood is over and mercy shall prevail.

**Crowd**    Mercy? That's no good to us

**Gentleman**    Yes, I promised the wife we'd take in a show.

*The* **Guard** *sings in West End musical style.*

**Guard**
No more beheadings, no more chains
No more whippings, no more dungeons

No more knocks and no more pain
No more lovely gory games.

*The* **Crowd** *applauds.* **Tom** *and* **Elizabeth** *sail past in the Royal Barge.*

**Crowd**
There he is.
Give us a wave, Edward.
He looks just like his poor dead muvver.
Shame about his sister Elizabeth.
Who d'you think designed his coronation gown?
Dunno. But they'll be flogging copies in the market by teatime.

*Elsewhere* **Miles** *and* **Edward** *arrive and tether the horse.*

**Miles**    The barge is heading for Westminster Abbey. We'll have to run along the Thames.

**Edward**    Come on, then! My crown is at stake.

*They run along the Thames as the barge docks and* **Tom** *steps forward.* **Ma Canty** *pushes forward and throws her arms around* **Tom***'s leg.*

**Ma Canty**    Tom! My darling boy. You're alive!

**Tom** *freezes.*

**Elizabeth**    Do you know this woman, Edward?

**Tom**    I do not.

**Tom** *shakes her off and moves on.* **Ma Canty** *weeps bitterly.*

**Ma Canty**    My own son and he won't acknowledge me. What did I do wrong?

**Crowd**
'Ere, listen to this one!
Beggar woman says the King's her little boy.
Now I've heard it all.

**Edward** *and* **Miles** *fight their way to the front.*

**Edward**    I heard you, good woman, and I believe you.

**Ma Canty**    Tom? (*She points at the real* **Tom**.) And Tom? What is this magic?

**Edward**    It is no magic. There is Tom Canty, dressed in my royal clothes. And here am I, Edward, who you cared for in Awful Court.

**Ma Canty** (*kneeling*)    Your Majesty.

**Miles**    Bless you for humouring his fancy, madam, but we cannot tarry here.

**Ma Canty**    It's no fancy, sir. That's my boy, I tell you, stepping through the arches of Westminster Abbey.

**Miles**    But it's impossible. That means – (*Out.*) That means –

**Edward**    It means I'm Edward the Sixth, King of all England.

**Miles** *kneels before* **Edward**.

**Miles**    Your Majesty, lord . . . if only I had known it . . .

**Edward**    You mean to say that all this time you thought I was making it up? I'll say this for you, Miles, you're very good at pretending.

**Miles**    Forgive me for disbelieving you, Your Majesty, I'm covered with shame. If only I had a bag to hide my head in.

**Ma Canty** *proffers a sack*.

**Ma Canty**    Here you go, love.

**Edward**    Arise, Sir Miles. Of course I forgive you.

*They embrace.* **Canty** *stumbles on*.

**Canty**    There you are, you little bleeder!

**Ma Canty**    Help! That's my husband!

**Edward**    Guard! He's a murderer!

**Guard**    Says who?

**Miles** *draws his sword with a flourish*.

**Miles**   Says I, Lord Hendon!

**Guard**   Fair enough, mate.

*The* **Guard** *grabs* **Canty** *and carries him off.*

**Edward**   Thank God. Now, how will we get into the Abbey?

**Miles**   Like this. (*He puts on* **Lady Edith***'s cloak.*) I'll pretend to be a priest.

**Ma Canty** *puts on her own cloak and beckons* **Edward***.*

**Ma Canty**   And we'll pretend to be a nun.

**Edward**   Anon.

**Ma Canty**   No, a nun.

**Miles**   Now run!


**Scene Twenty-Five**

*Westminster Abbey.* **Tom** *walks slowly up the red carpet to the altar where the* **Archbishop** *waits with* **Hertford** *and* **Elizabeth***. A choir sings.*

**Choir**
  Welcome O King, as much as hearts can think
  Welcome again, as much as tongue can tell
  Welcome to joyous tongues and hearts that will not shrink
  God thee preserve, we pray and wish you well

  Approach O King, on this momentous day
  Approach again, upon the royal throne
  Once the crown is on your noble head
  What's done is done, and for ever set in stone.

**Tom** *has reached the throne and is seated.*

**Archbishop**   Cheer up, Your Majesty. This is a day for celebration, not misery. If you look ill on your people, they will take it as a bad omen.

**Tom**    But I'm wicked, Archbishop. I just turned my back on my own dear mother.

**Archbishop**    Dear God. His malady has returned!

**Hertford**    Nonetheless, he must be crowned. Perhaps it is better to have a mad king with a kind heart than a sane tyrant.

*As the* **Archbishop** *raises the crown above* **Tom***'s head,* **Edward***,* **Miles** *and* **Ma Canty** *race towards the altar.*

**Miles**    In the name of King Edward – stop!

**Edward**    The crown belongs on my head, not his!

**Hertford**    Guard!

*A* **Guard** *moves in to seize* **Edward***, but* **Tom** *stands.*

**Tom**    Wait! (*To* **Edward**.) Let him go. He's telling the truth!

**Edward**    At last!

**Tom**    A minute, Your Majesty. (*He goes to his mother.*) Oh, Ma, please forgive me. I thought only to be king and make this country better. I didn't mean to deny you.

**Ma Canty**    It's all right, son. Your father won't hurt you no more. He's in prison for the rent collector's murder.

**Tom** *and* **Ma Canty** *embrace.*

**Archbishop**    What in the name of holy water is going on?

**Edward**    It's very simple, Archbishop. We swapped clothes and were mistaken for each other. Only this boy wouldn't give up the game.

**Elizabeth**    That's impossible! A pauper has not governed the country this last week!

**Miles**    Yes, he has. And rather well by the sounds of it.

**Tom** (*to* **Edward**)    I tried to tell them who I was, my lord, but they wouldn't listen. So I thought I'd better make the best of it.

**Edward**    So I see. (*To all.*) Well? Why do you not kneel before me? I am the rightful king.

**Archbishop**    The boys are as alike as twins, it's true. But how do we know which of them *is* the real king?

**Hertford**    Only the rightful King of England would possess the Royal Seal.

**Tom**    But the Royal Seal is lost.

**Edward**    The Royal Seal is not lost.

**All**    What?

**Edward**    Father told me to hide it somewhere until I became king, so I did.

**All**    Where?

**Edward**    In a suit of armour in my chambers.

**All** (*to* **Tom**)    Well?

**Tom** *brings out the Seal.*

**Tom**    Is this it? But you said it was a nutcracker.

**All**    A nutcracker?

**Tom**    No wonder it didn't work.

**Tom** *gives the Seal to* **Edward***.*

**Hertford**    Then truly, sire, you are our king.

**Miles**    Honour is restored and the future of the country saved.

**Archbishop**    Whatever. Now throw that pauper and his mother into jail. They'll hang for this monstrous treason.

**Edward**    Wait a minute. Surely their fate is up to me.

*He steps towards* **Tom***.* **Miles** *takes* **Edward** *aside.*

**Miles**    My lord, have you learned nothing on your adventures about the need for mercy?

**Edward**    Tom Canty . . .

**Tom** (*quaking*)    Yes, Your Majesty.

**Edward**    I could hardly have done things better myself. You and your family shall have the throne's protection and the crown's support.

*Everyone sighs with relief.*

**Tom**    Thank you, Your Majesty. I'll never try kinging again.

**Edward**    My father once told me that only fear might keep a country united. But he was wrong. I've seen charity from beggars without food or shelter, friendship from prisoners and peasants who saw only a poor boy in need. And in Miles Hendon, sacrifice beyond all duty. Princes or paupers, we are nothing without human kindness. Now put the crown on, for heaven's sake, and let's go to the banquet.

**All**    Long live King Edward!

*Song: 'What an England We Could Be'*

**Busker**
    Oh kind people, we bid you all good night
    Our tale is told, our work is done, we've set the world
      to rights
    Our message is quite simple, we hope you will agree
    With mercy and forgiveness

**All**
    What an England we could be
    How light and free our hearts feel, with no punishment
      or blame
    How light and free our lives would be if we only shared
      the aim
    To live and love together in our variety
    With mercy and forgiveness
    What an England we could be

**Tom/Edward**
    If you'll just try it out
    In time you'll recognise
    That there's no difference between

**Busker**
 A busker and Sir Miles

**Archbishop**
 A beggar and a priest

**Ma Canty**
 A mother and a chancellor

**Canty**
 A villain and a king

**Hertford**
 A servant and a lord

**Elizabeth**
 A princess and a pauper

**Tom / Edward**
 Two birds who can sing

**All**
 Oh kind people, embrace your enemy
 For kind people, he's just like you and me
 So walk along together
 And help each other see
 With mercy and forgiveness
 What an England we could be
 What an England we could be.